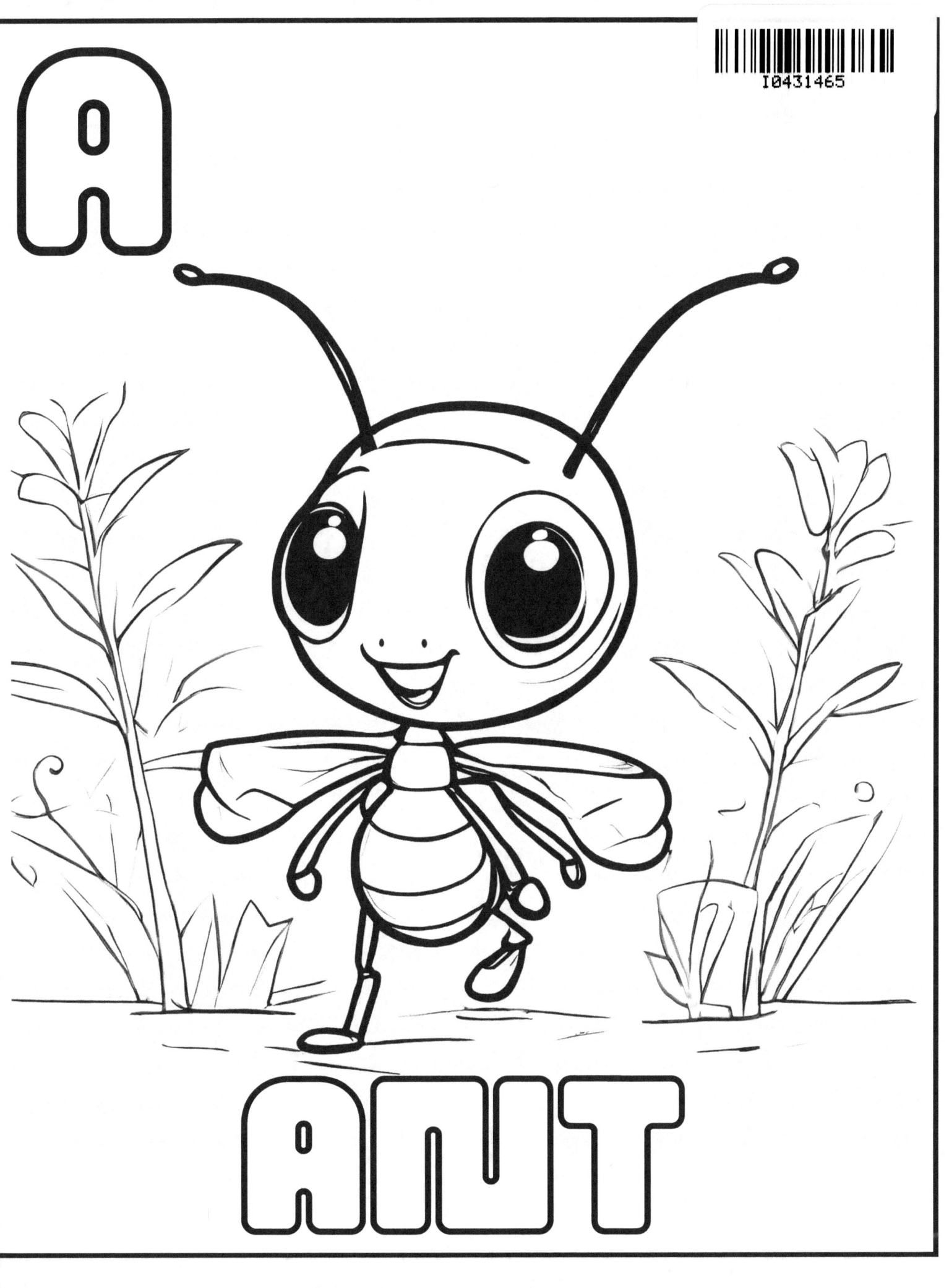

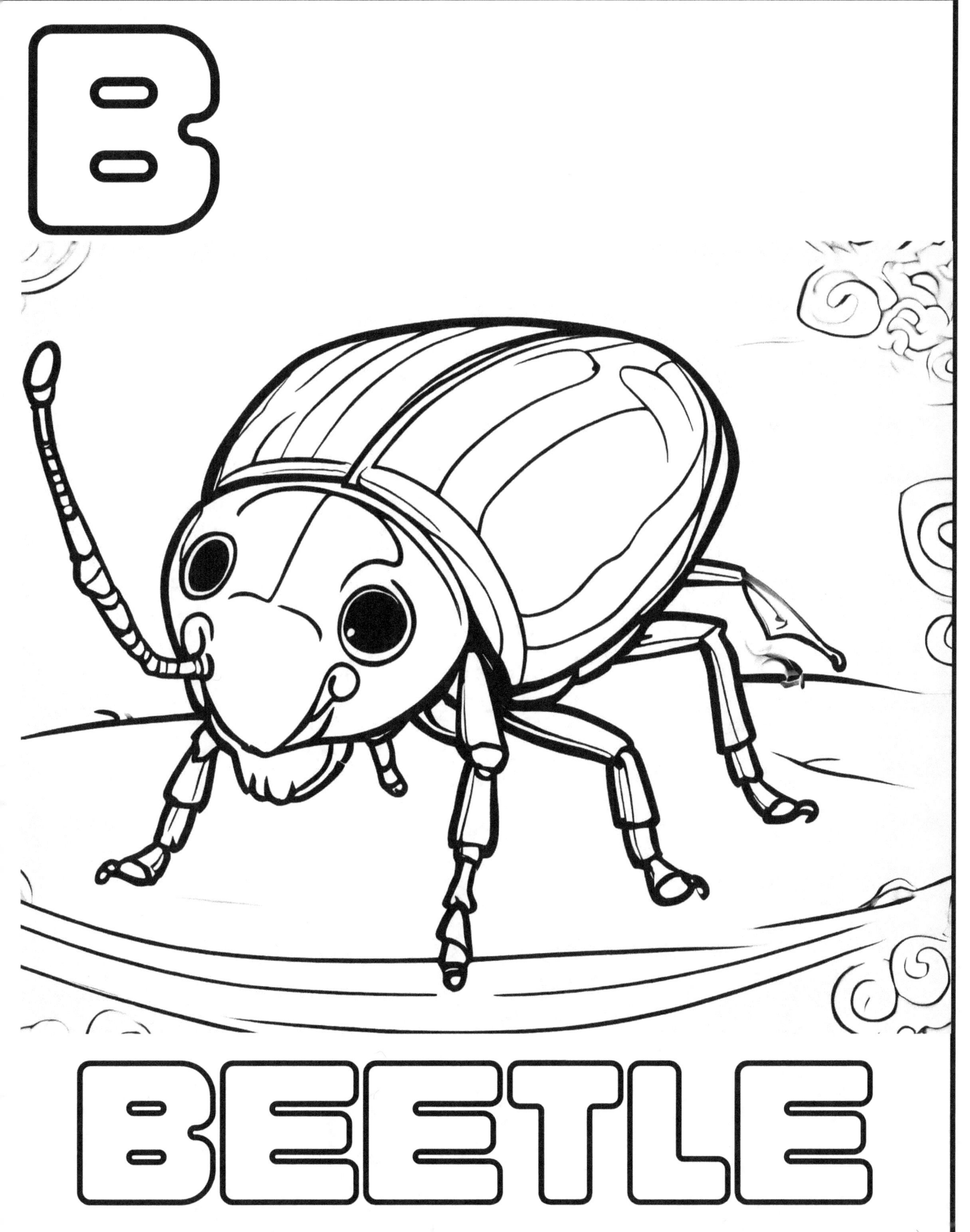

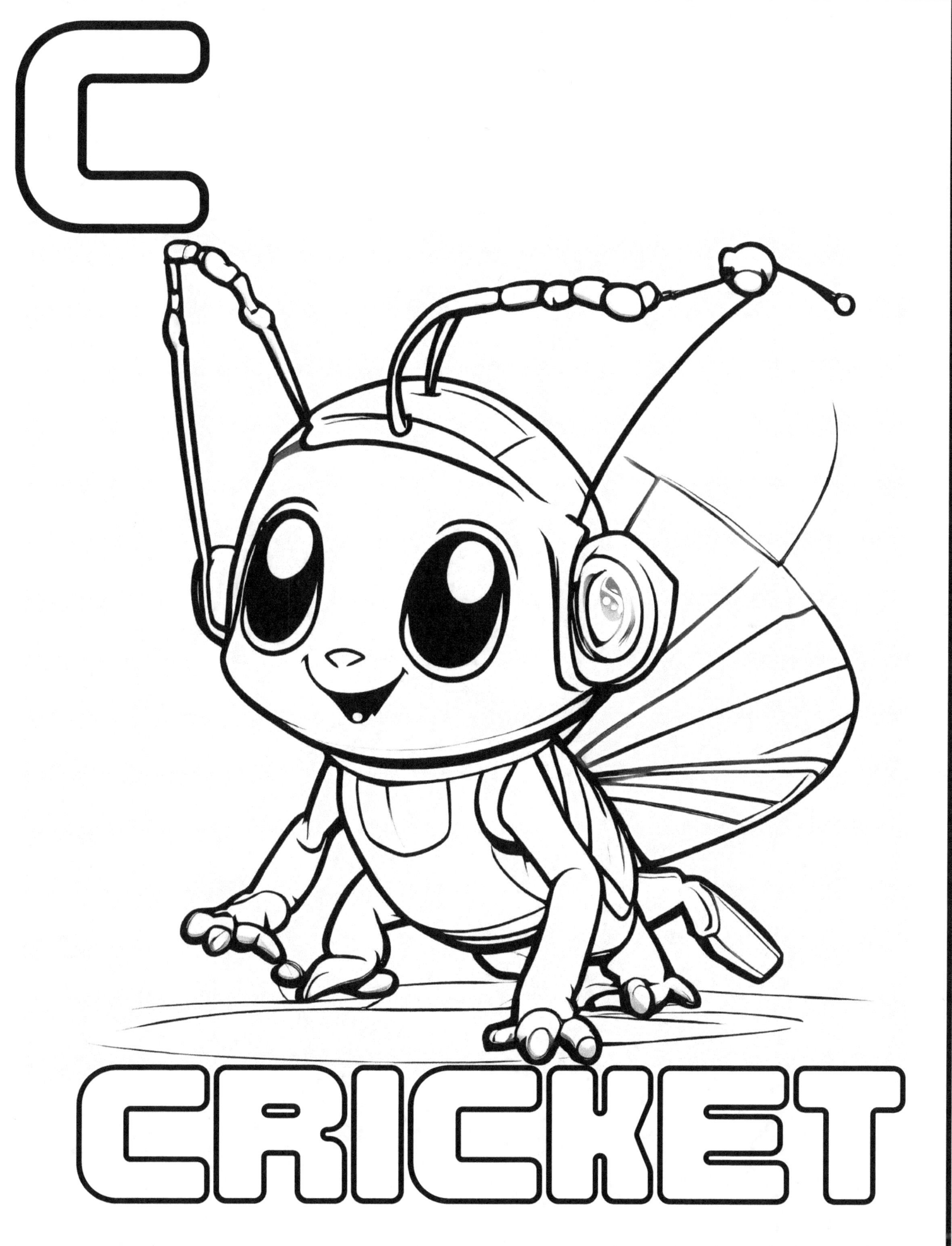

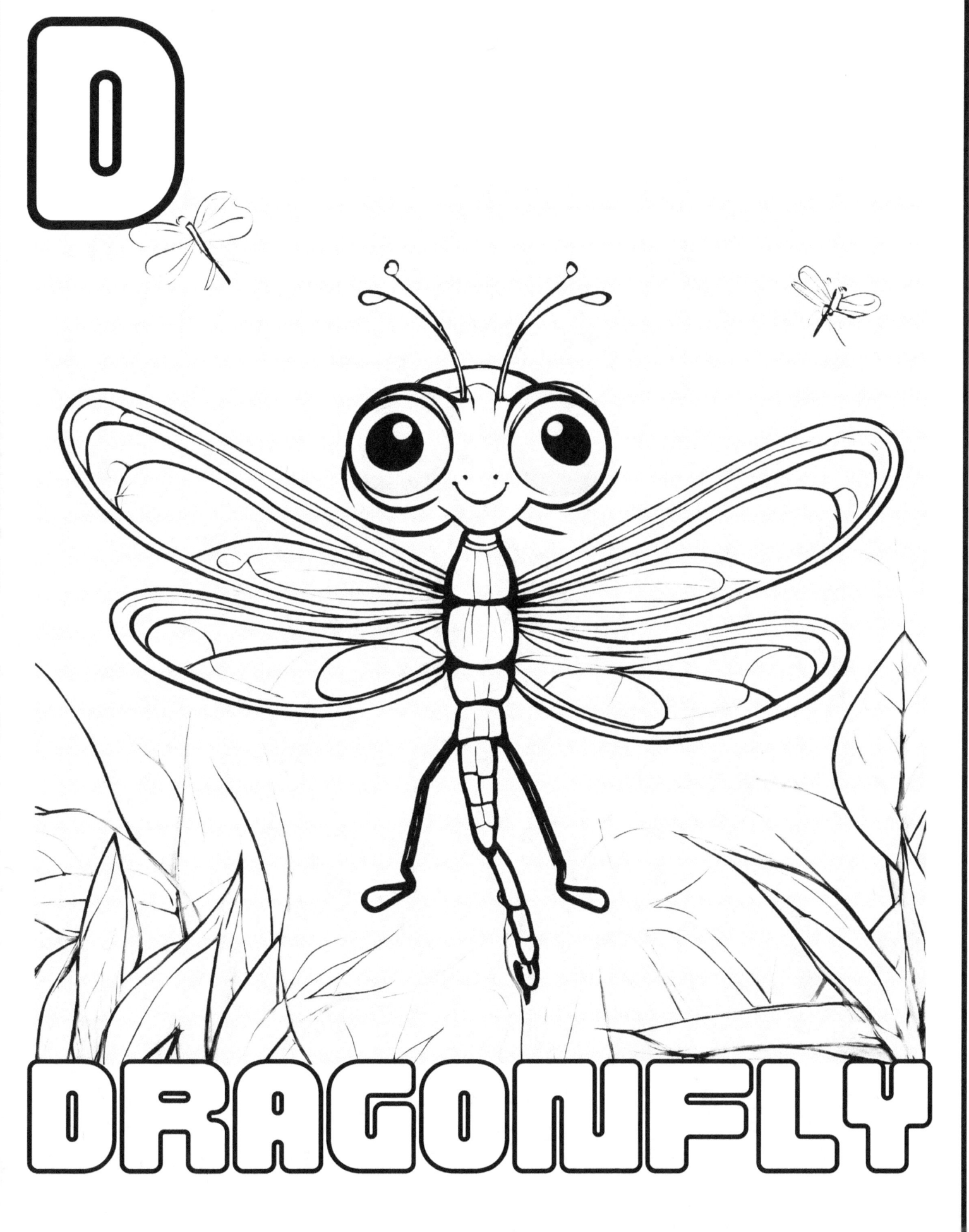

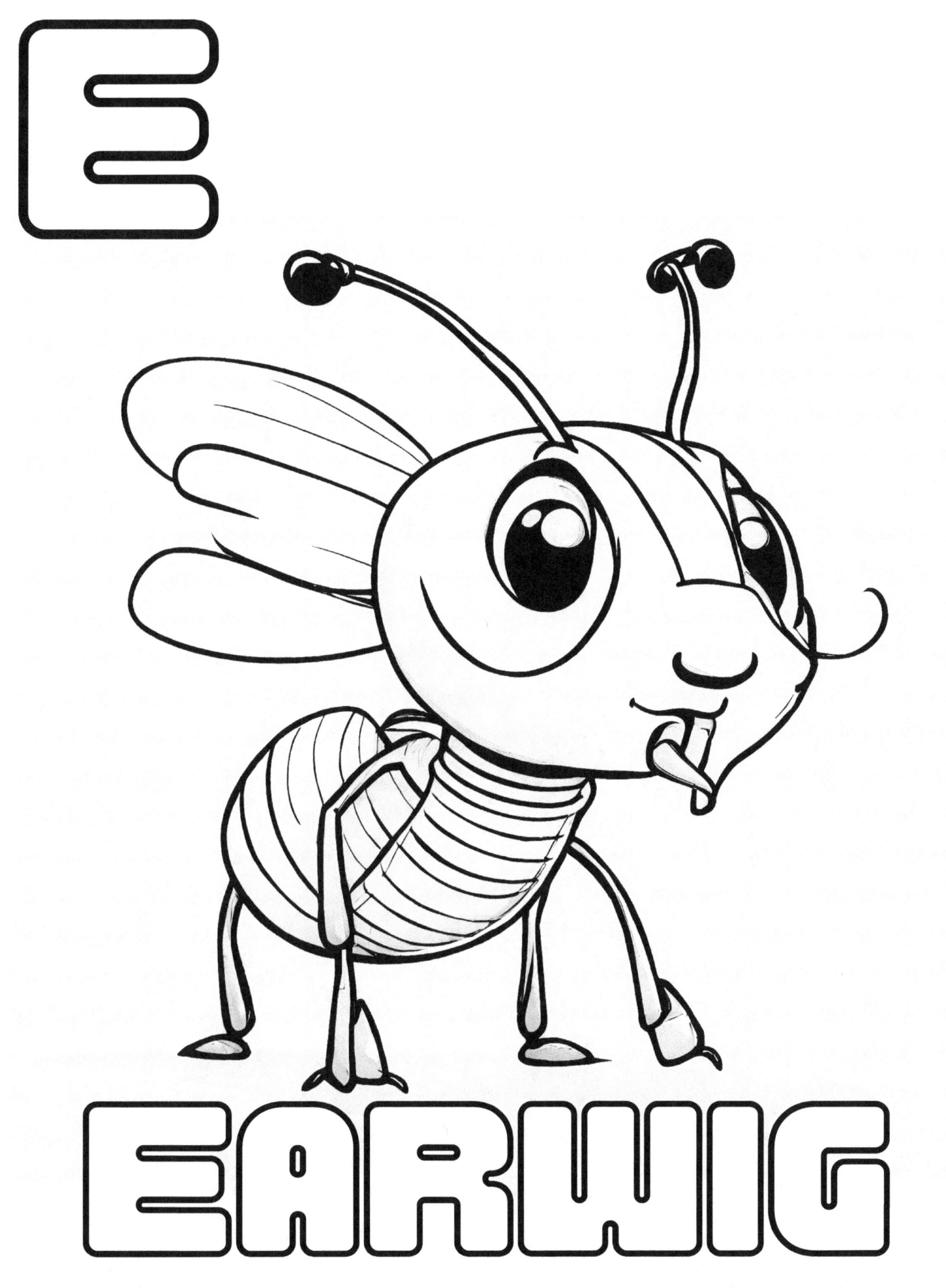

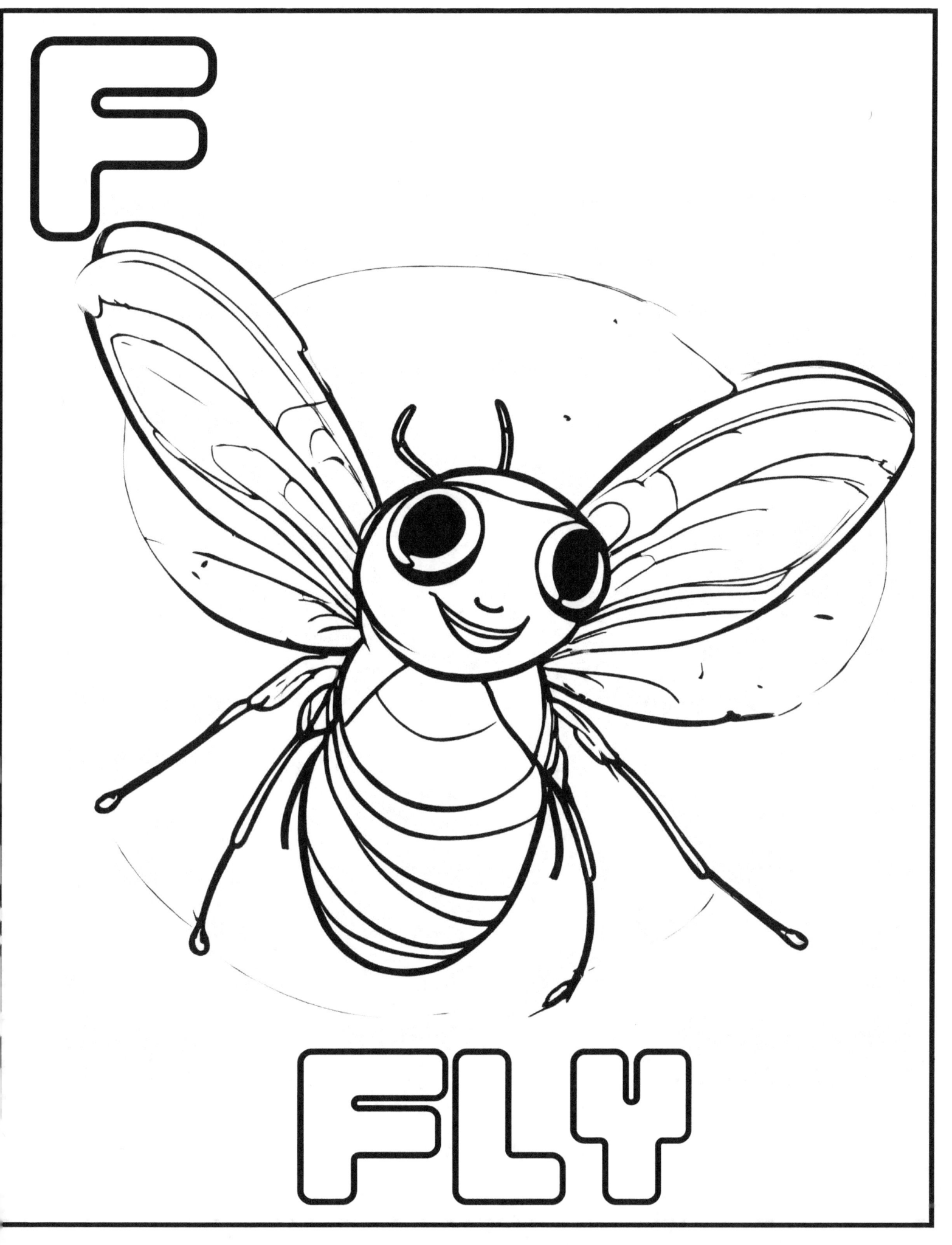

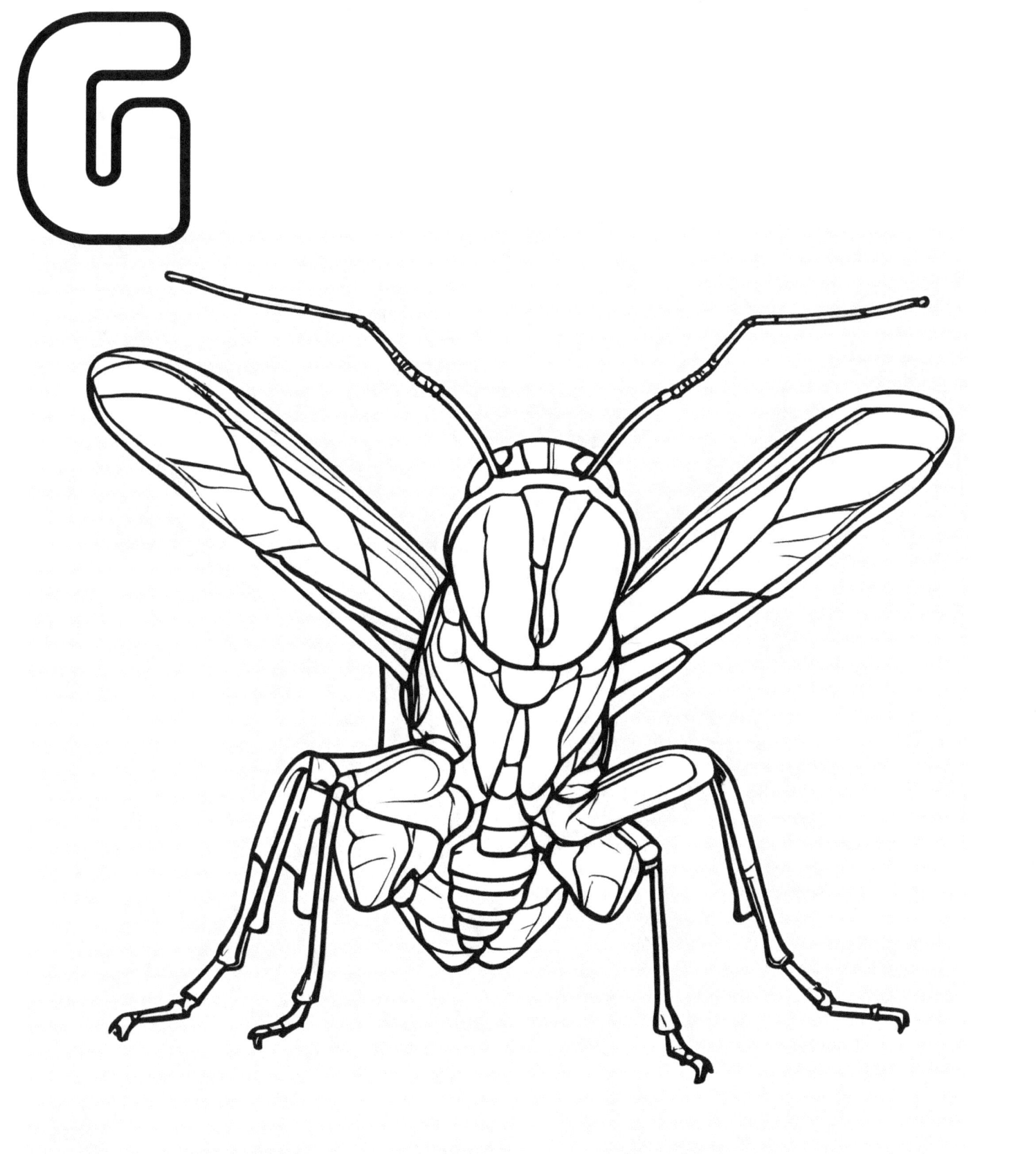

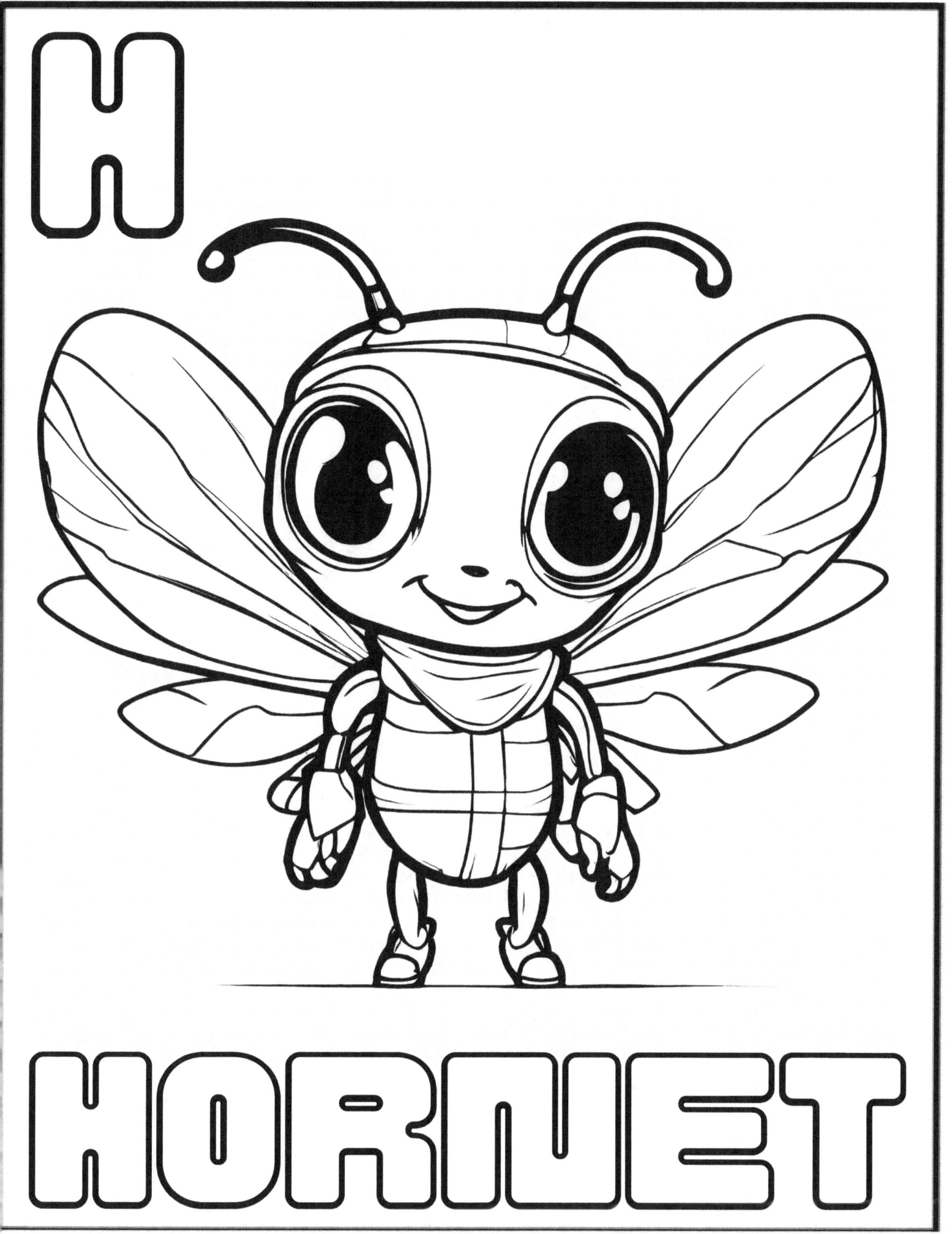

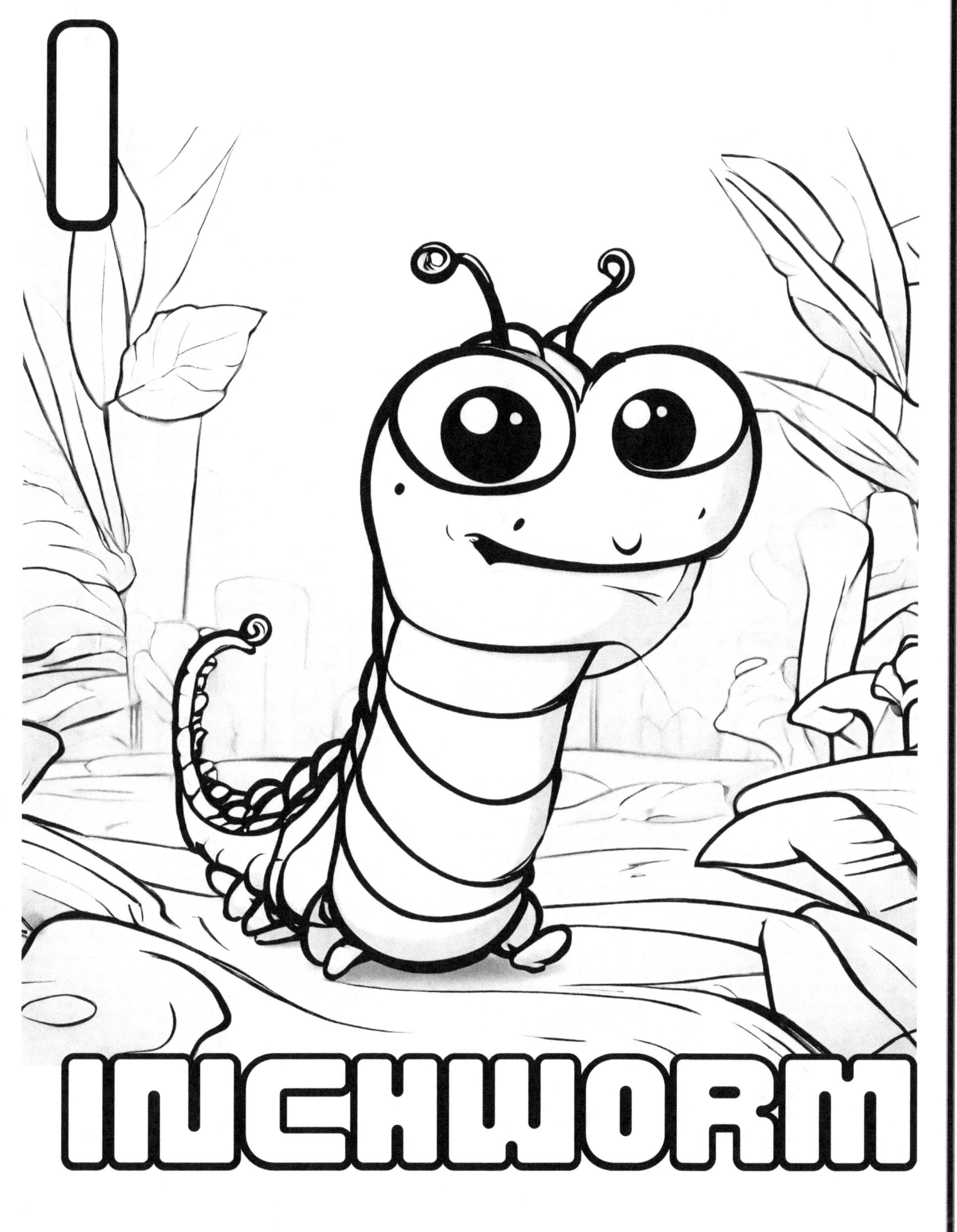

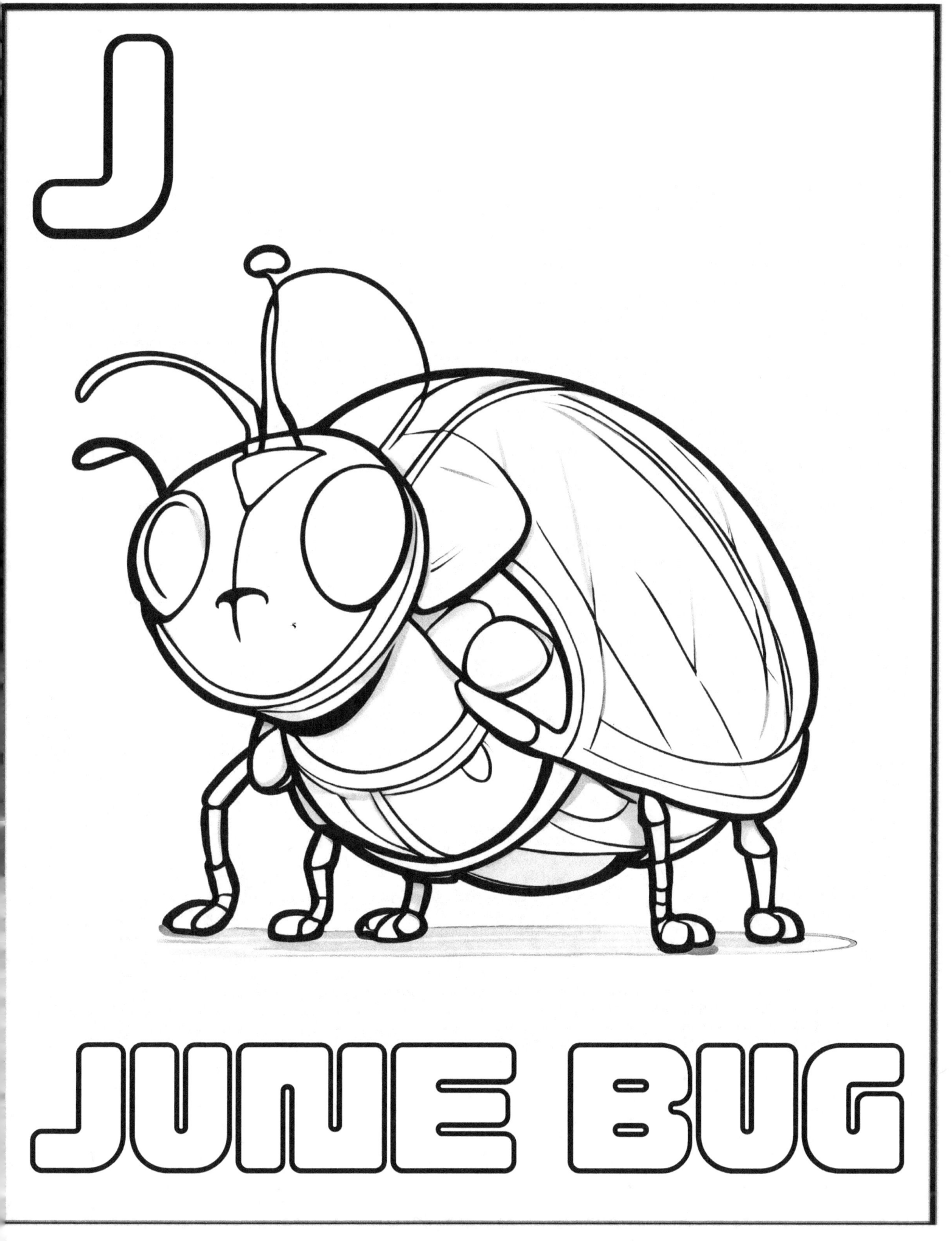

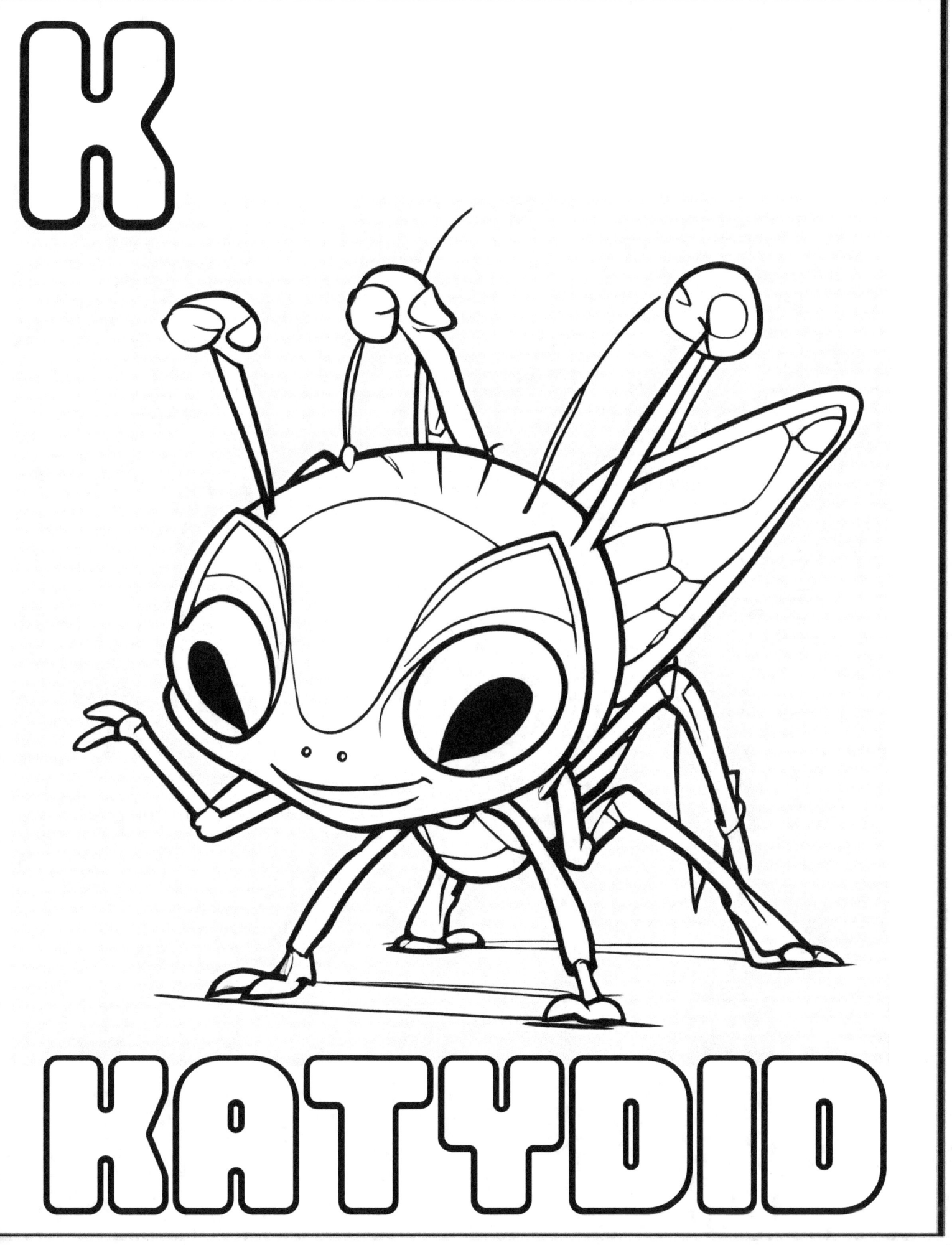

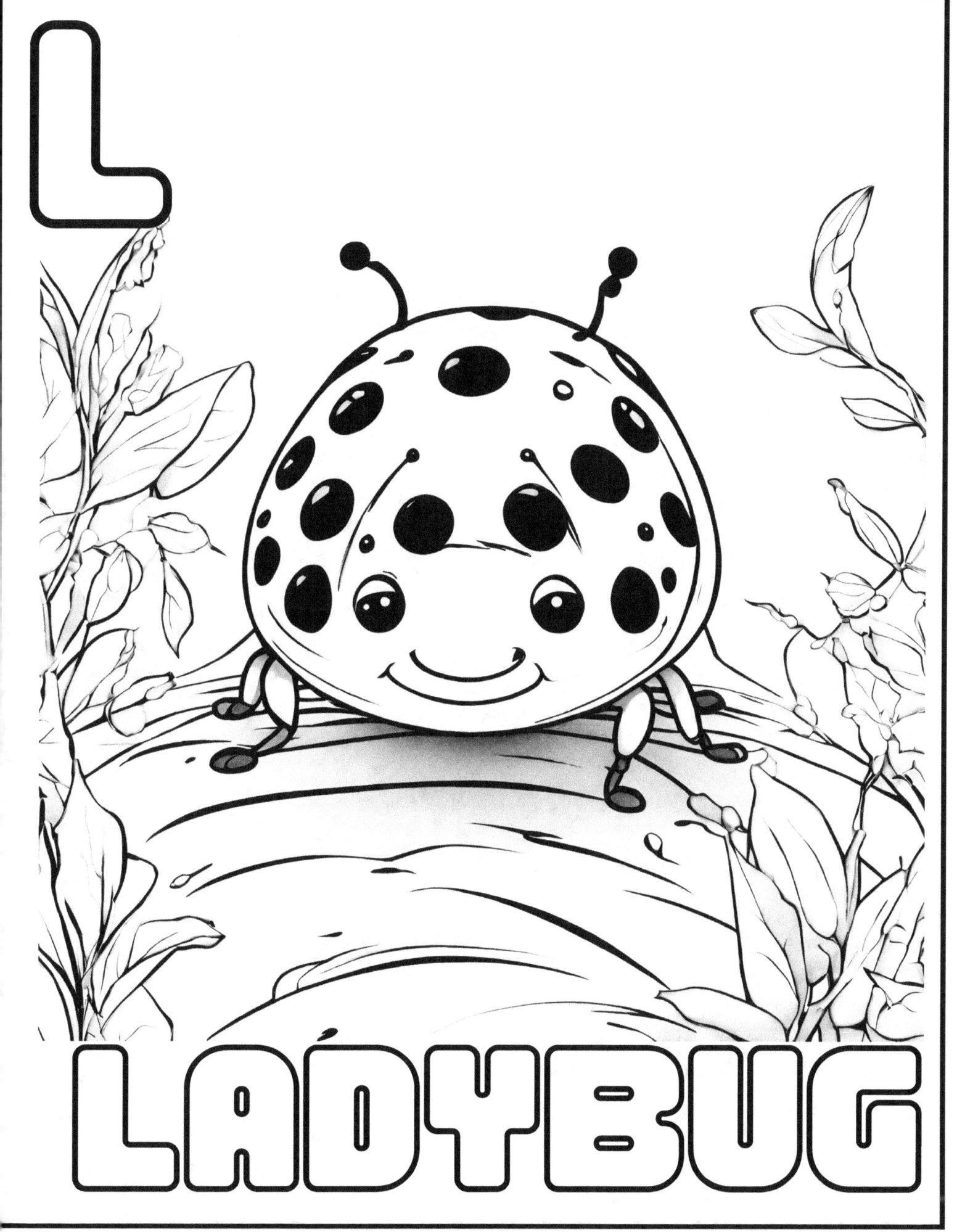

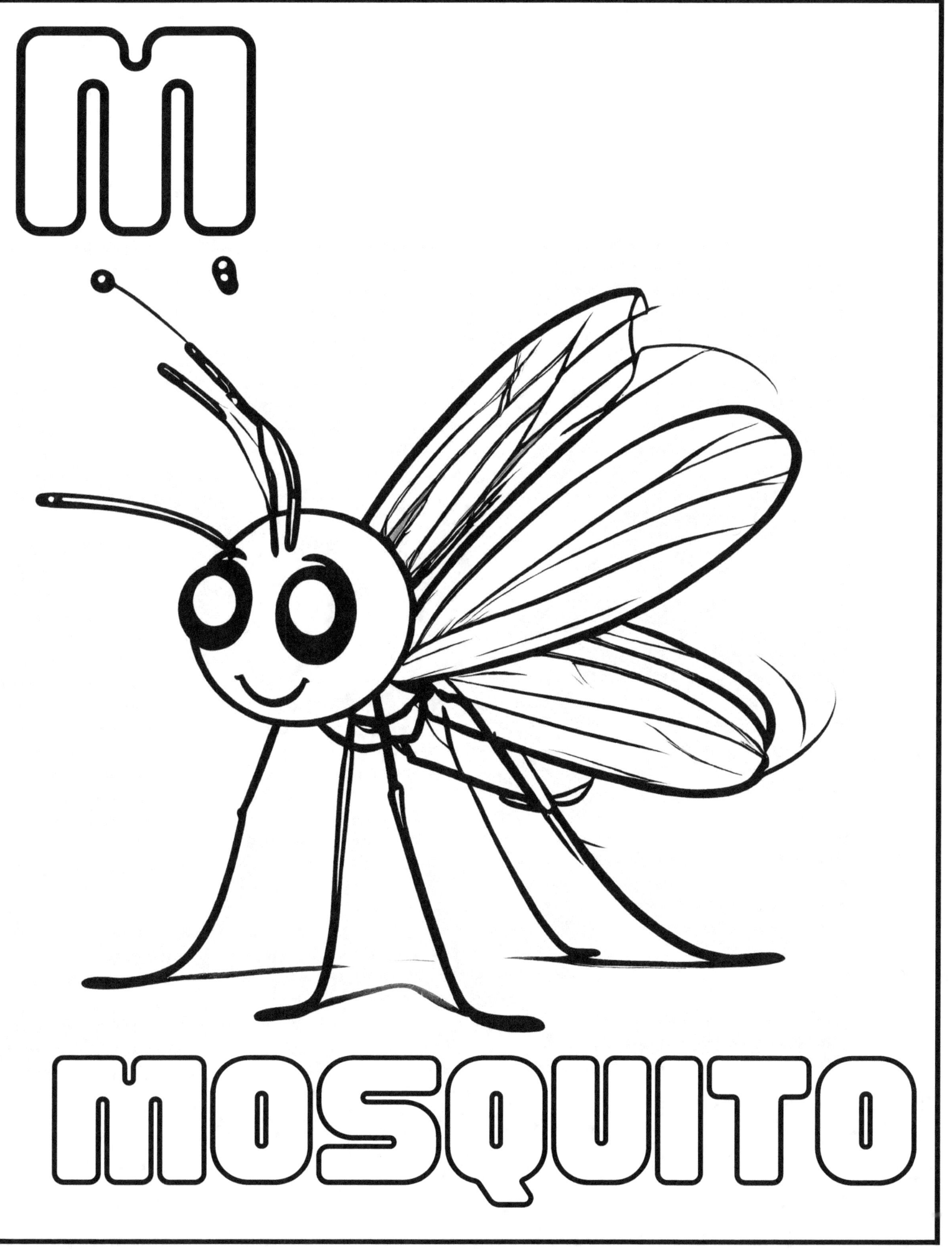

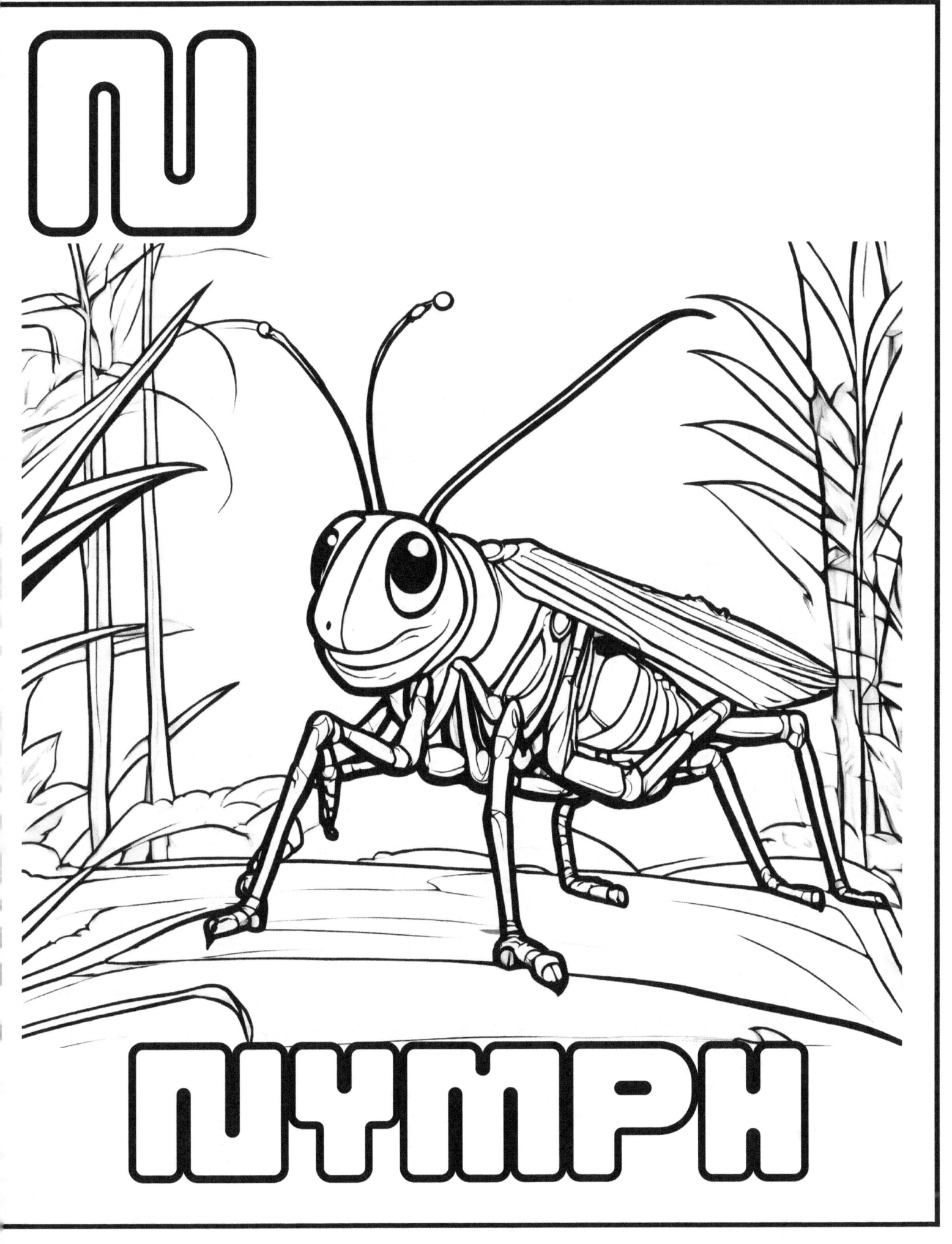

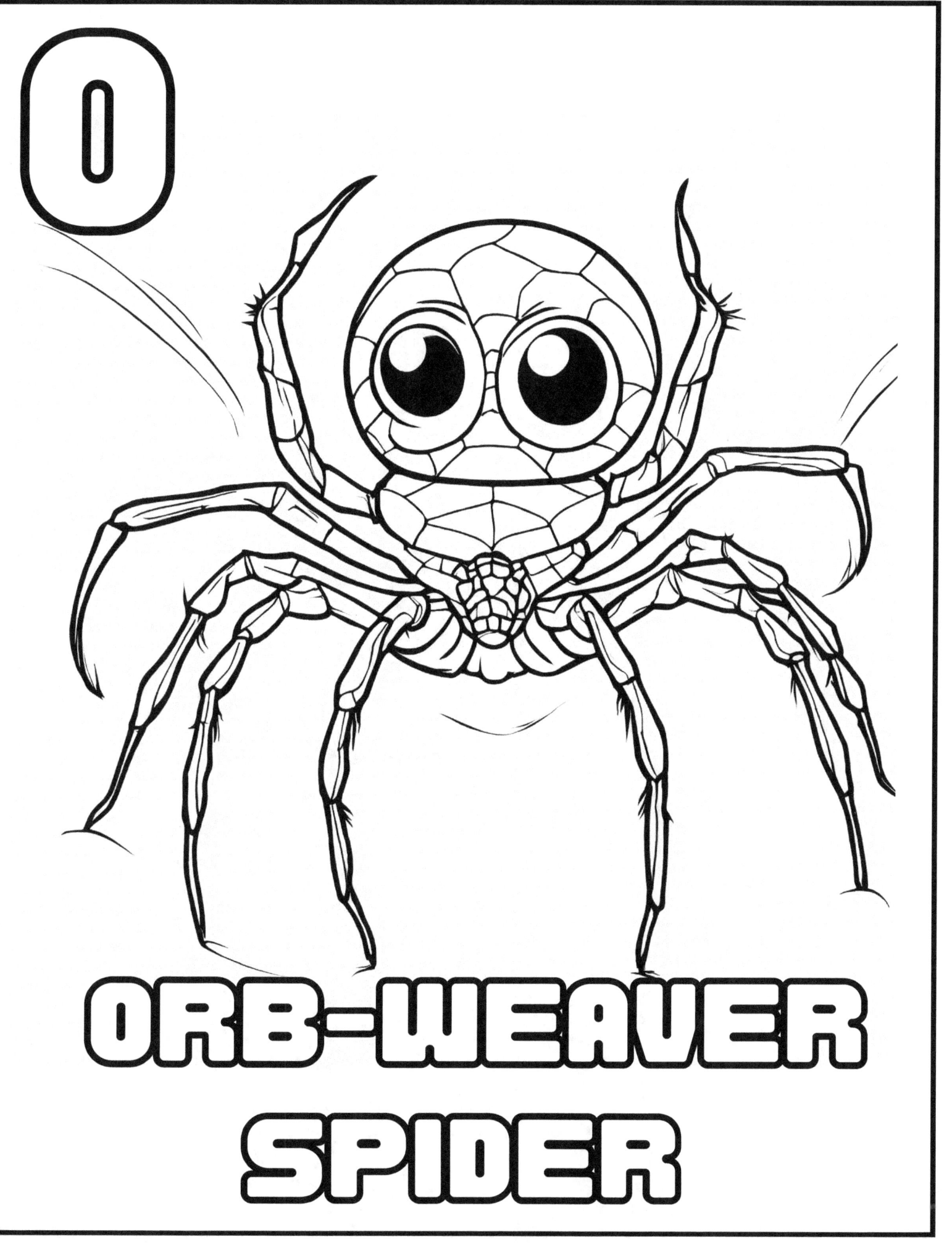

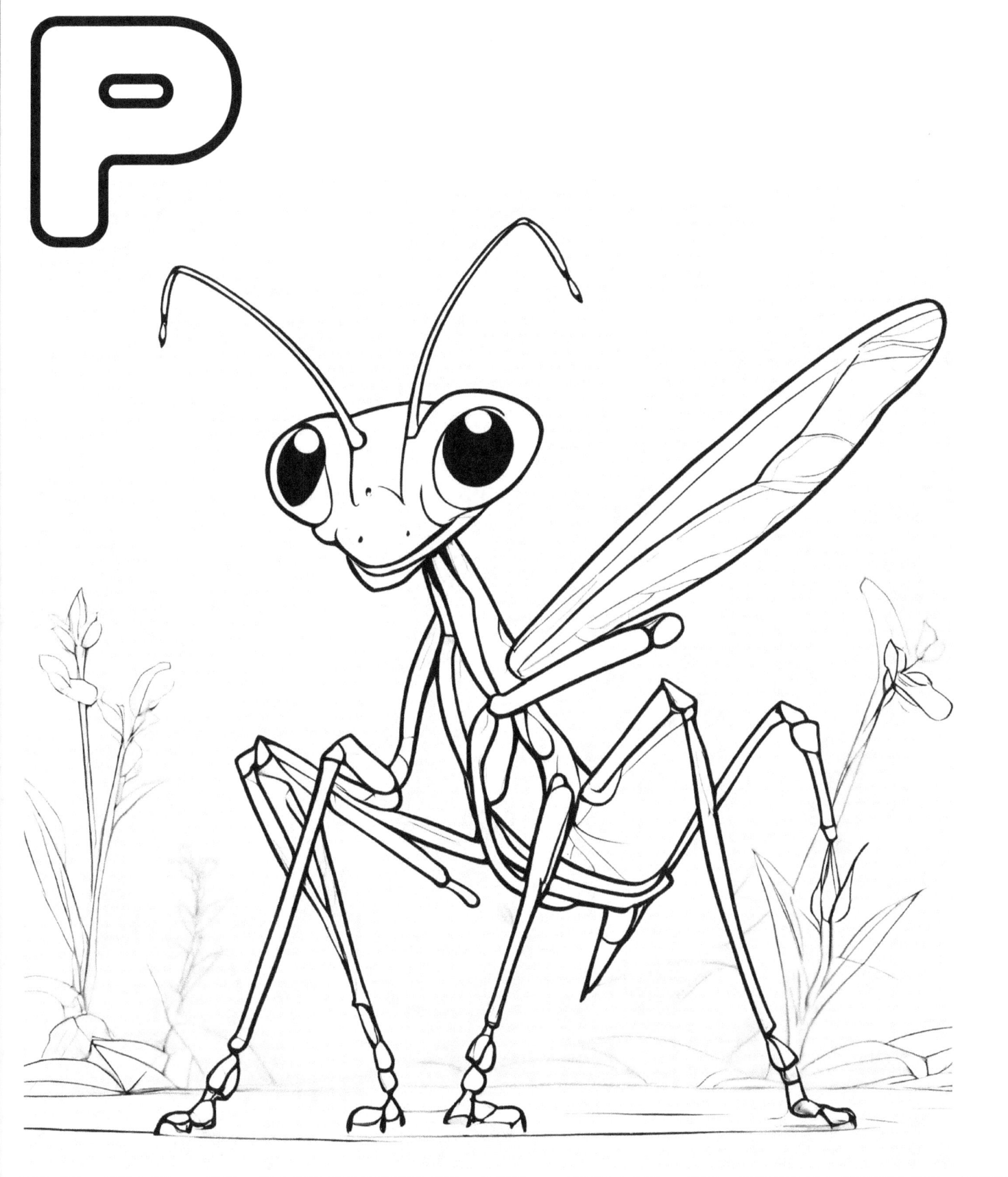

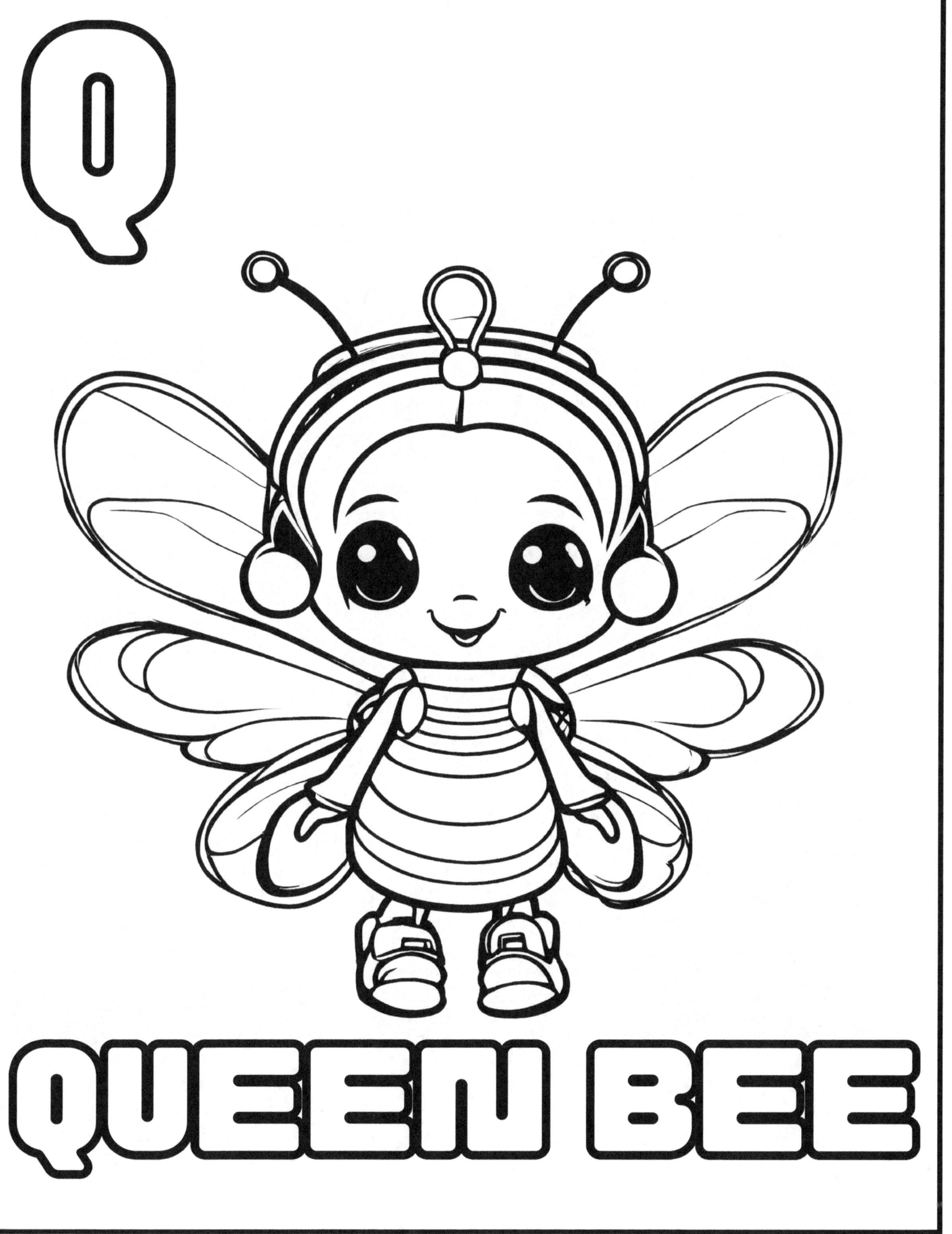

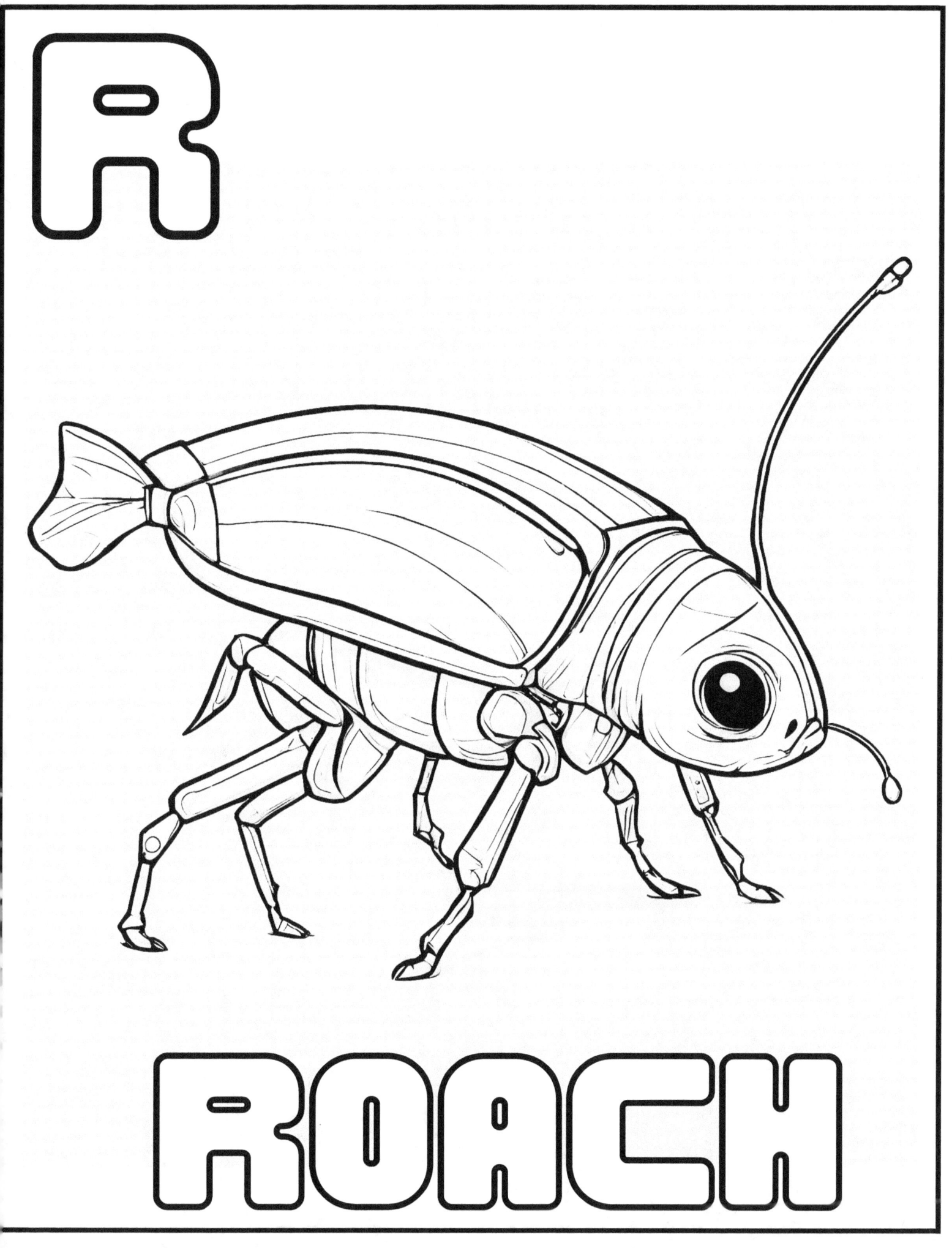

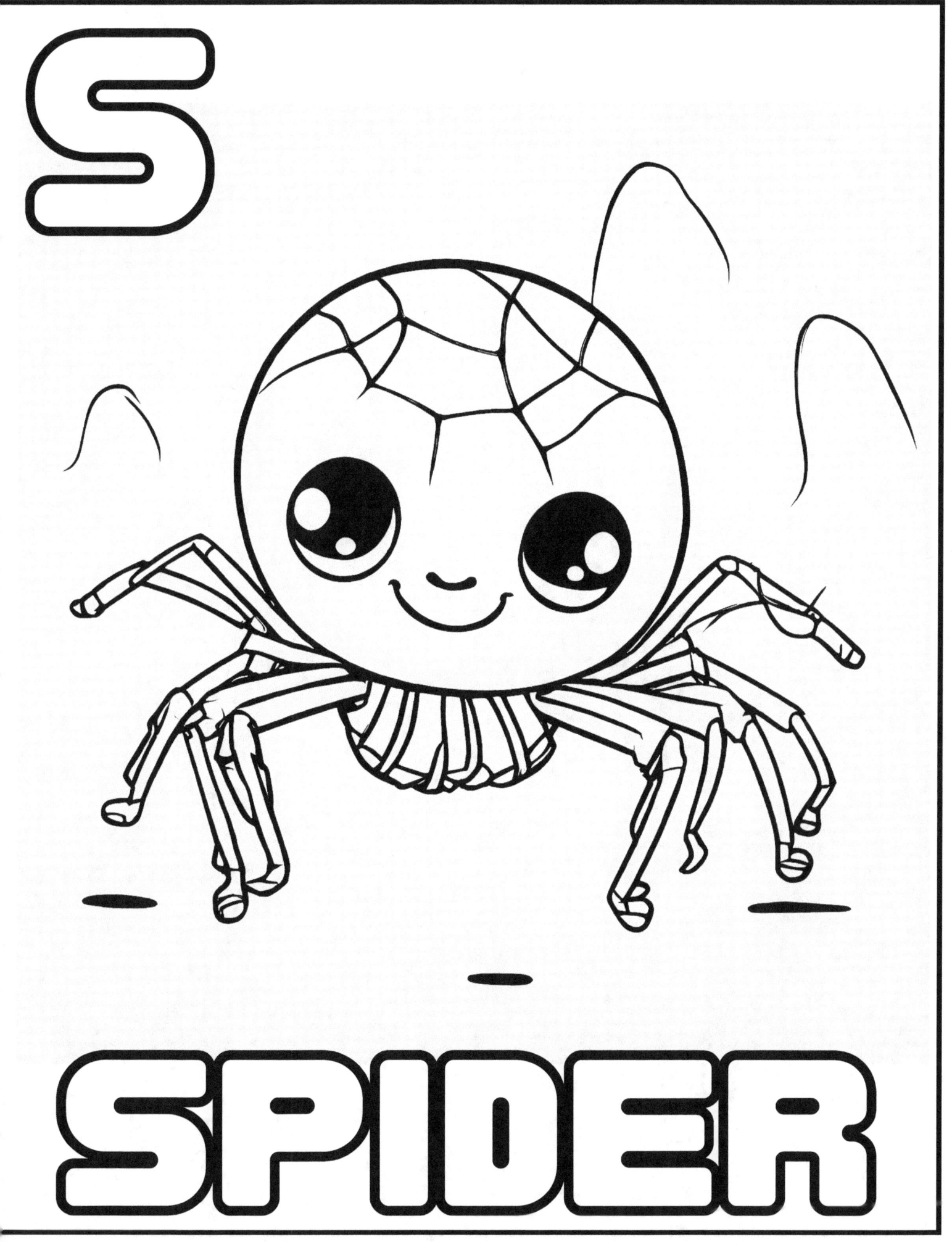

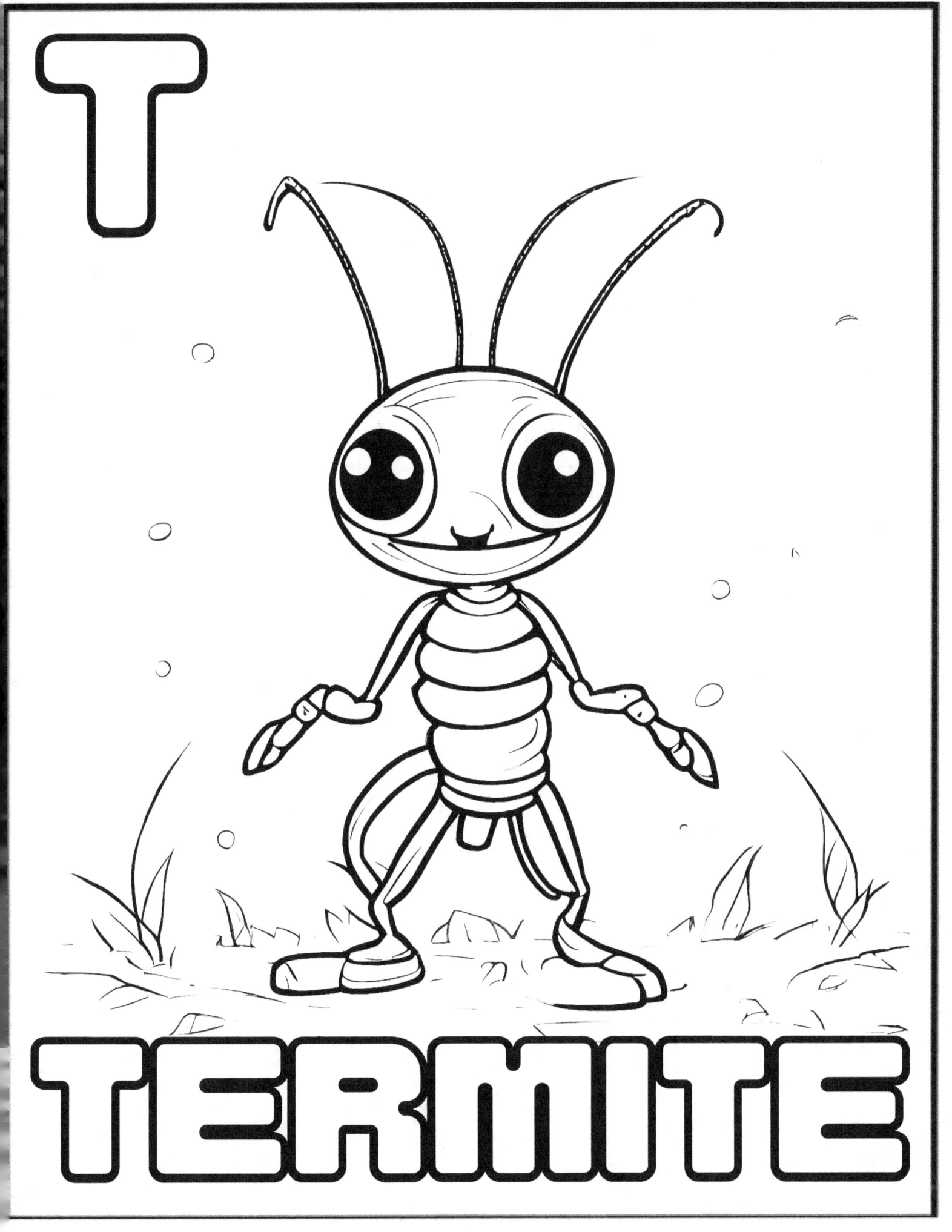

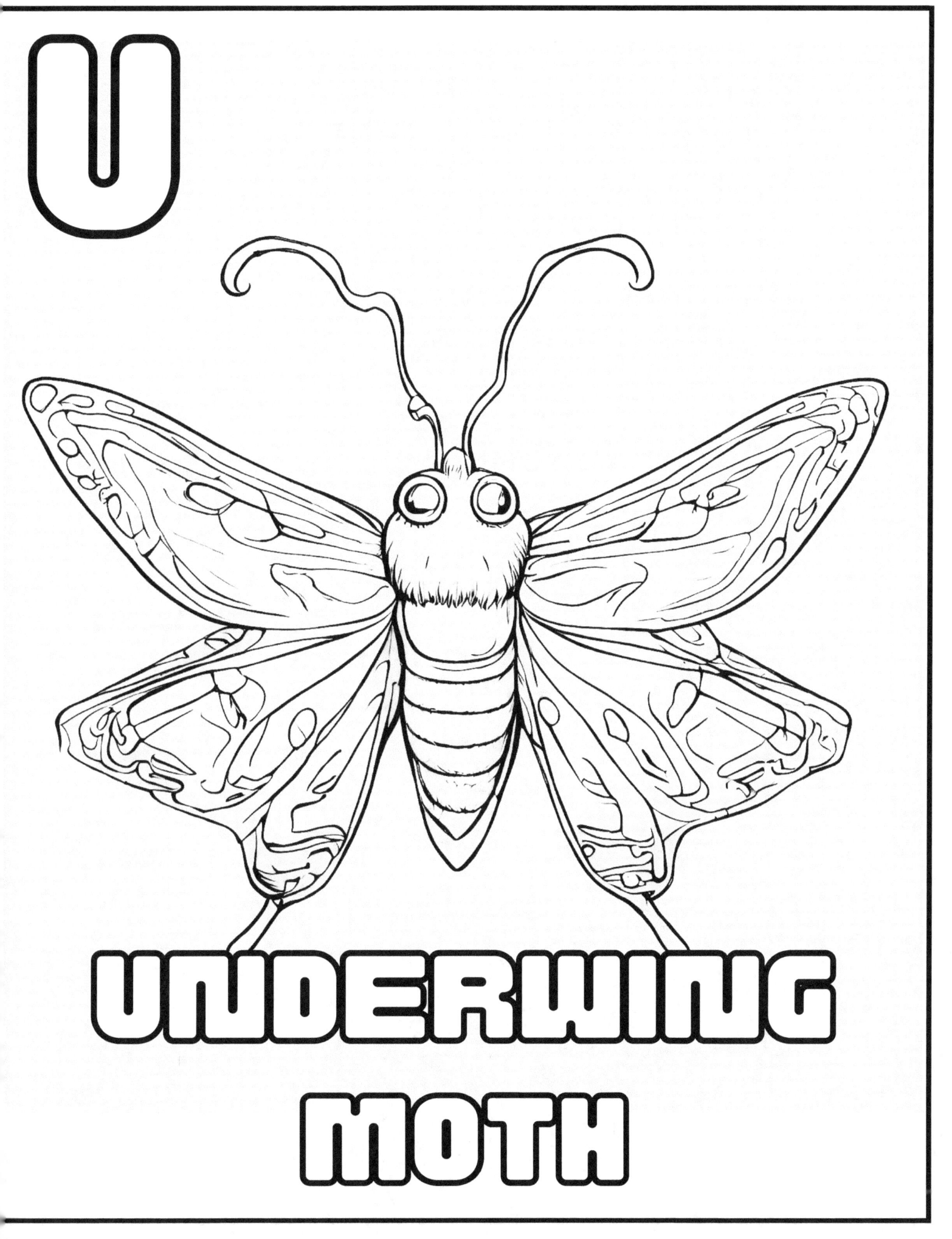

V

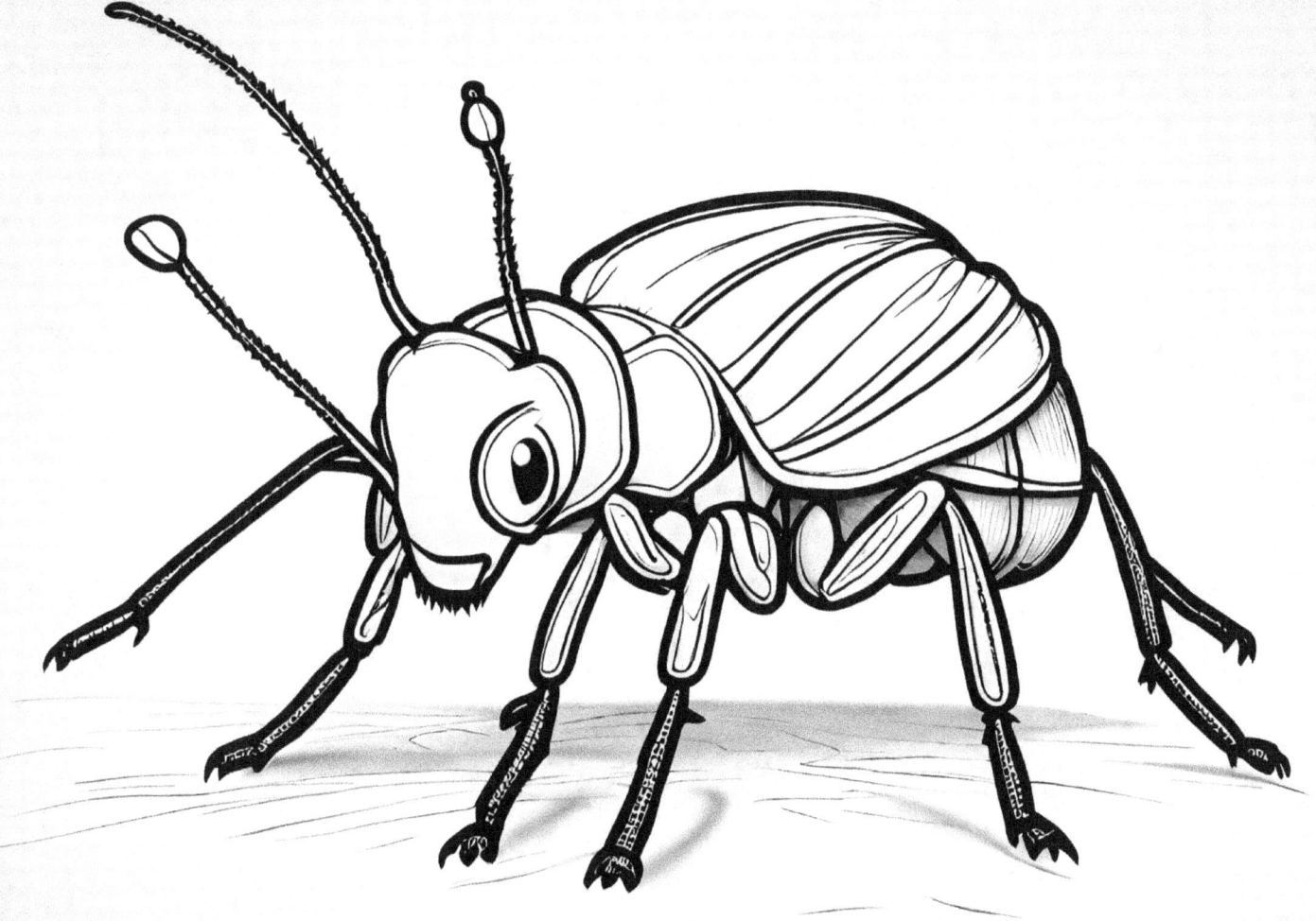

VELVET ANT

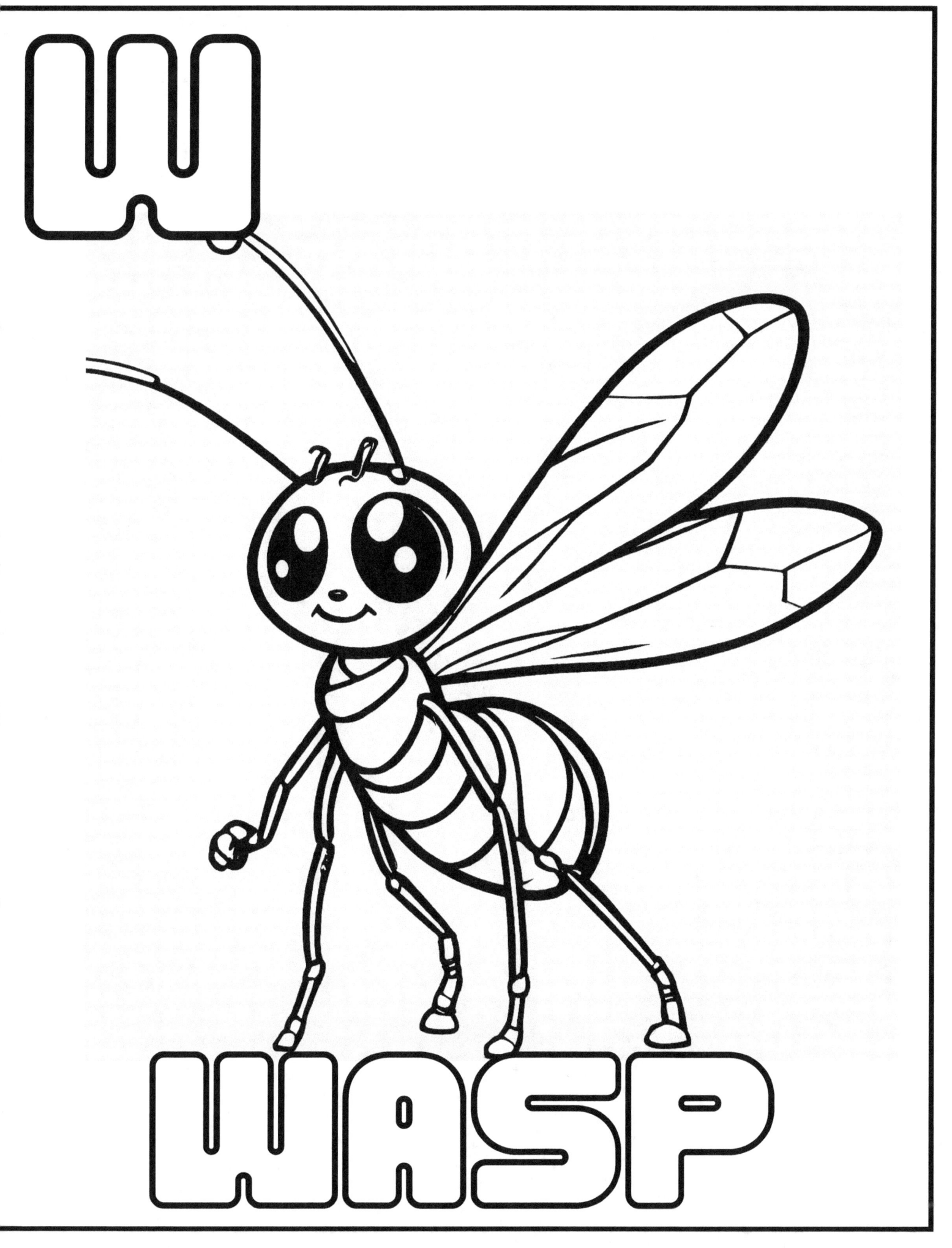

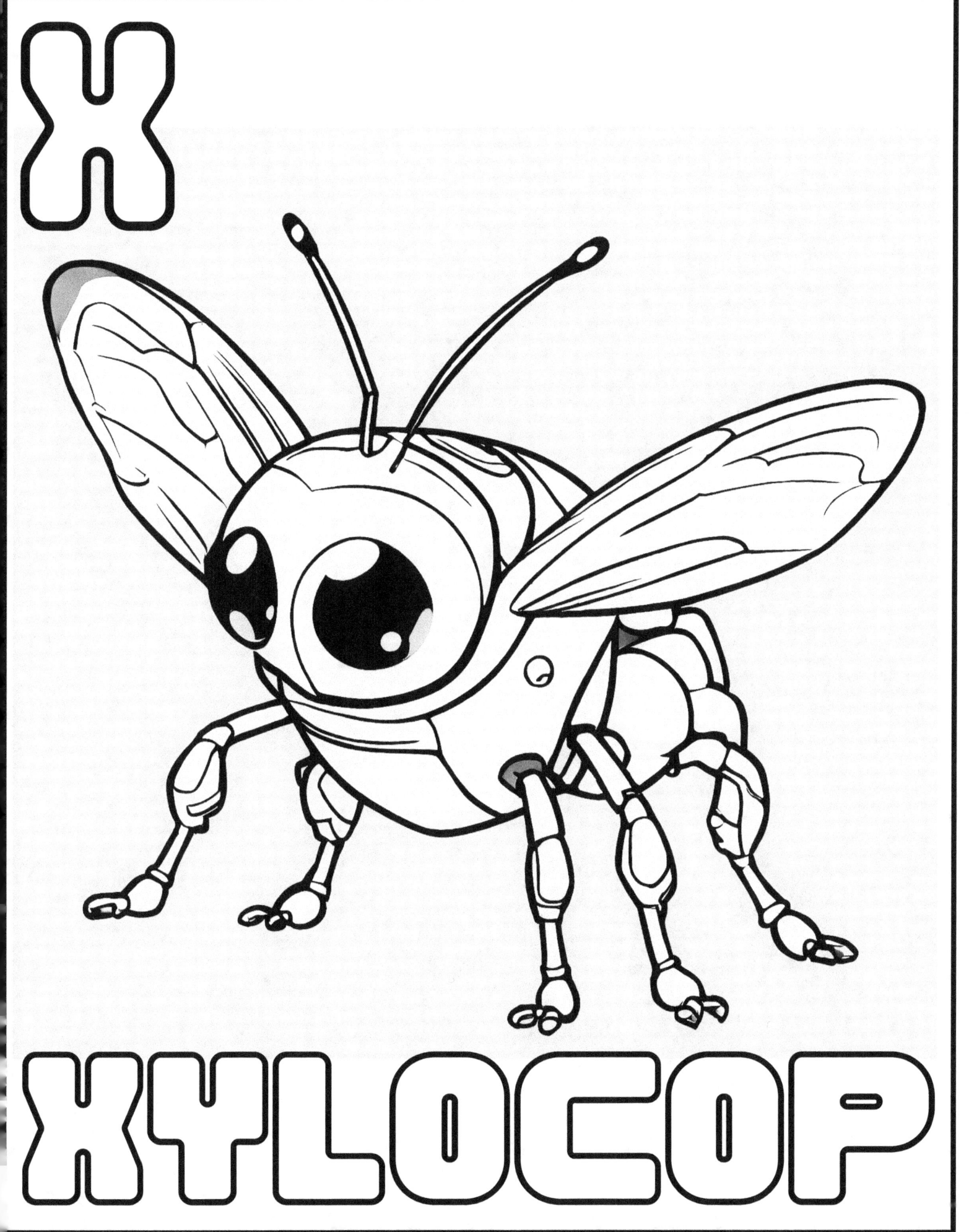

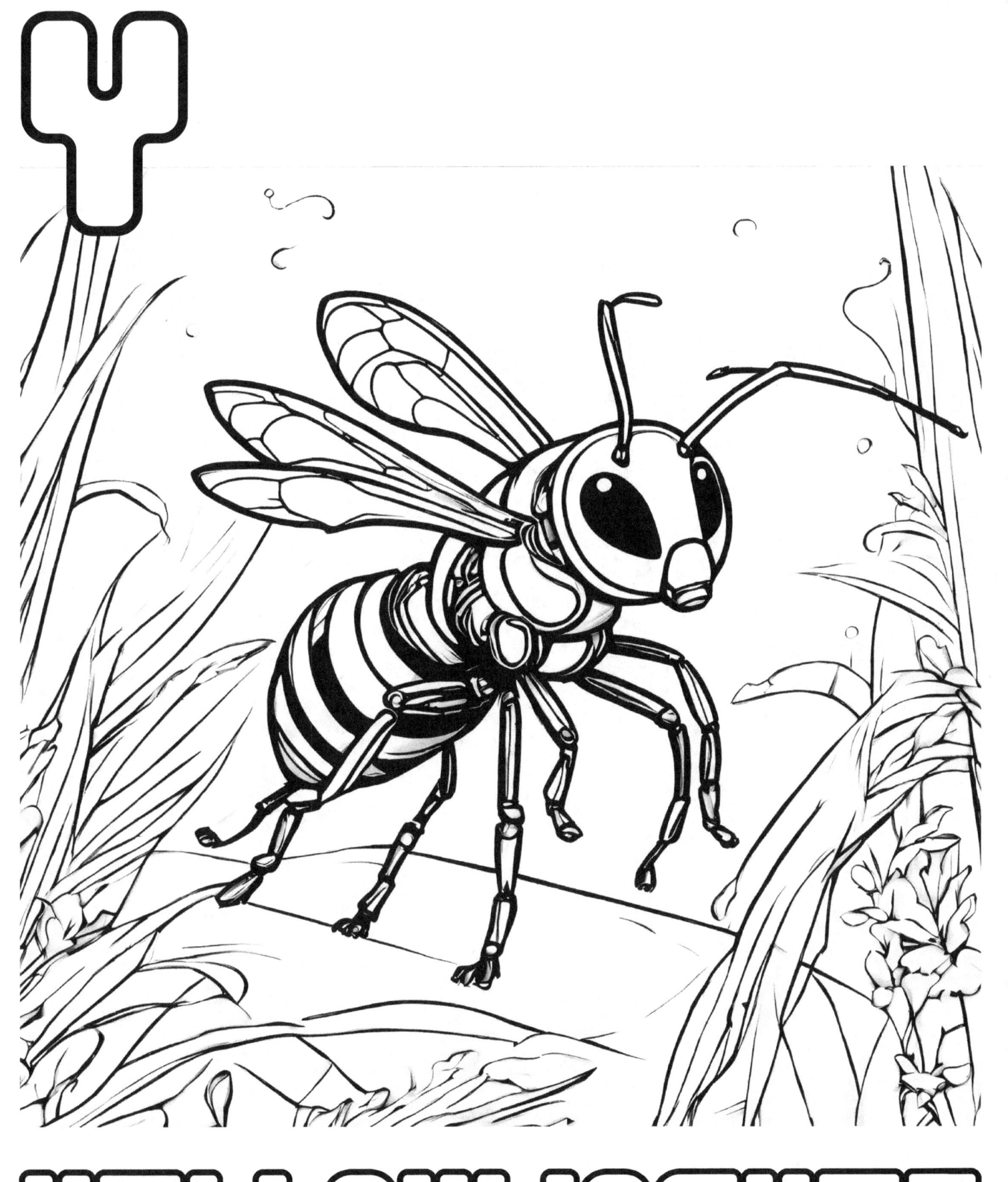

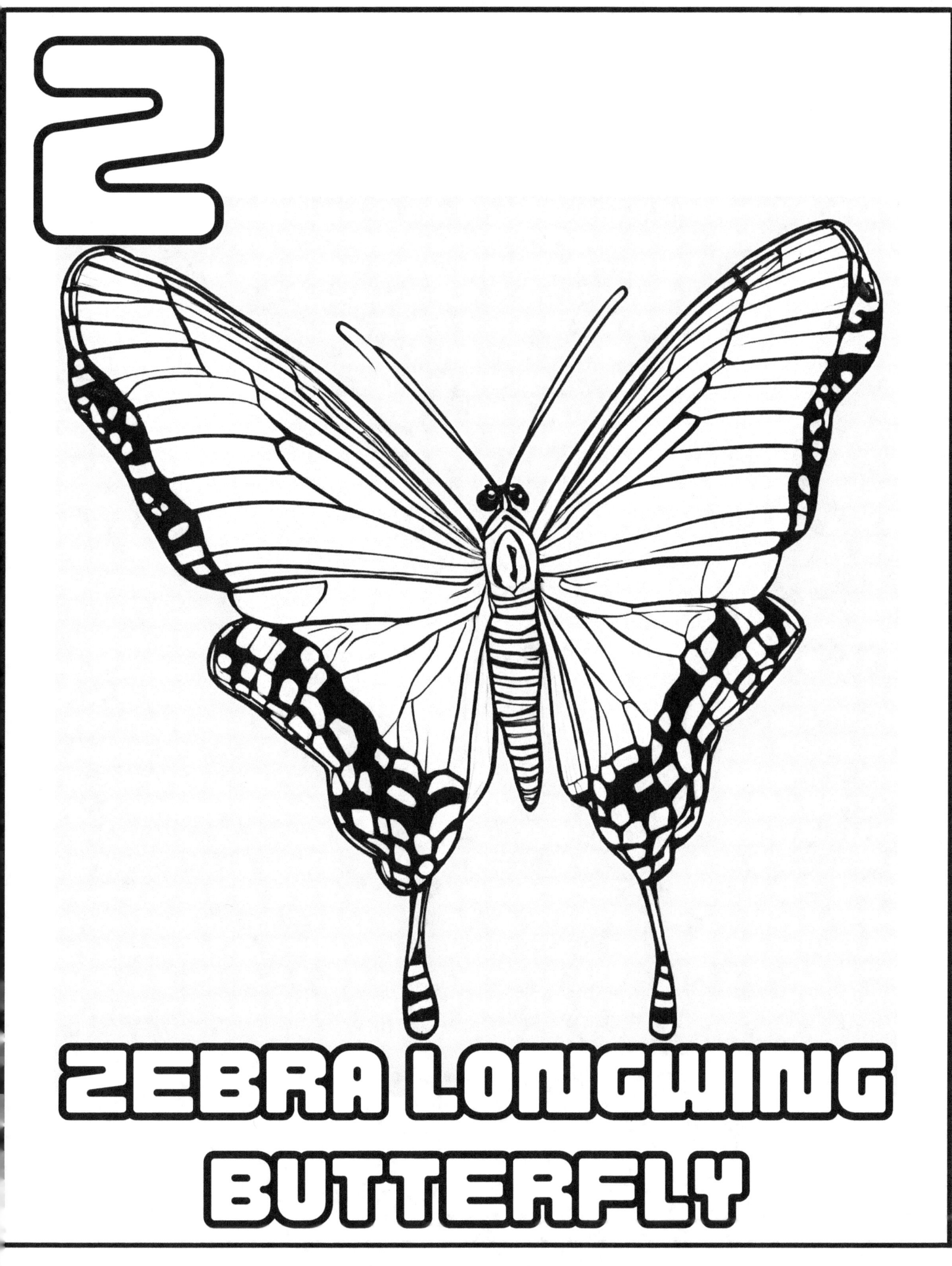

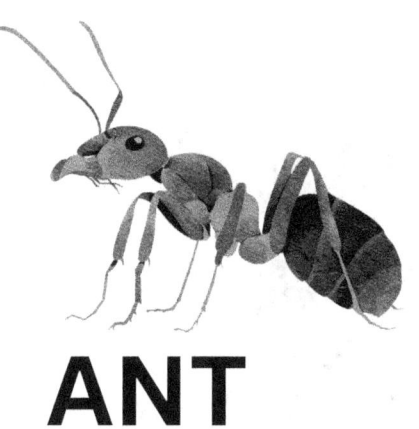
ANT

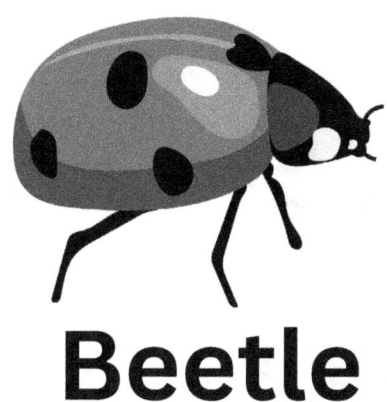
Beetle

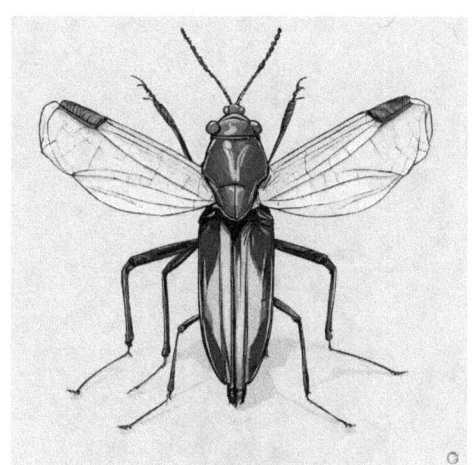
Cricket

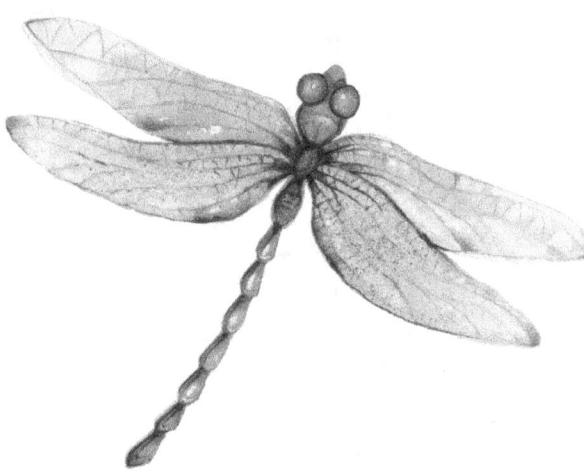
Dragonfly

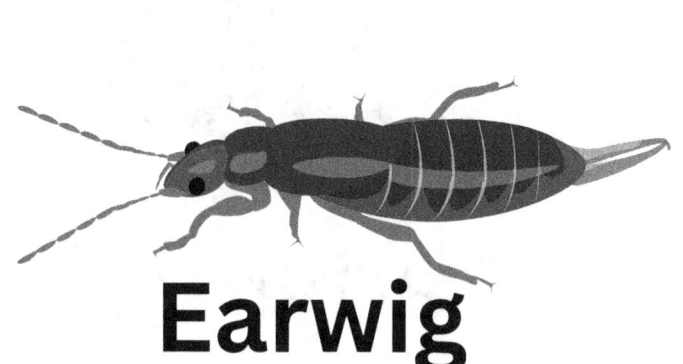
Earwig

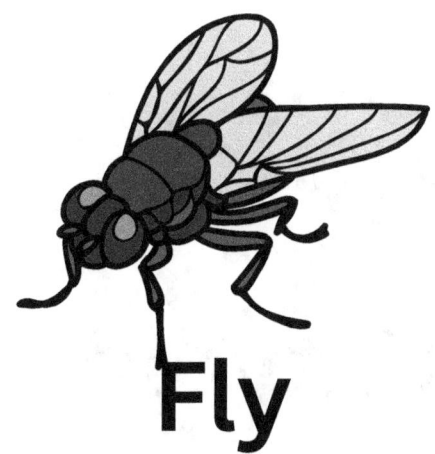
Fly

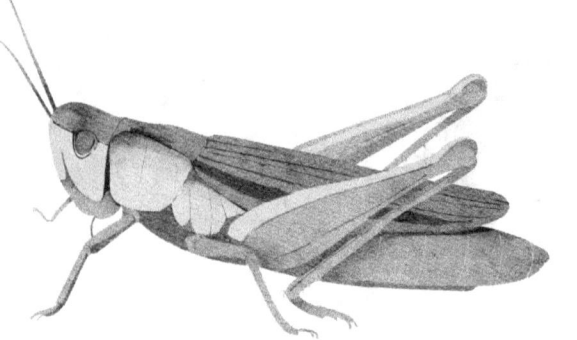
Grasshopper

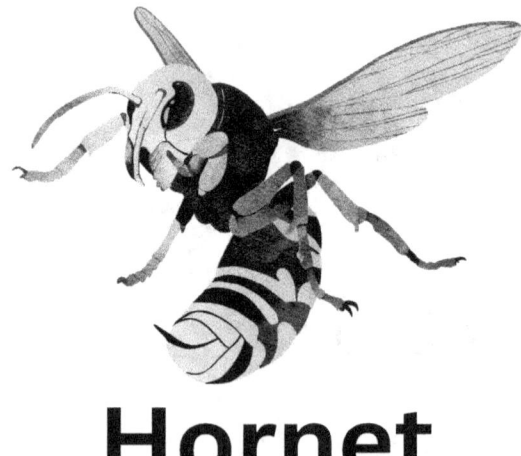
Hornet

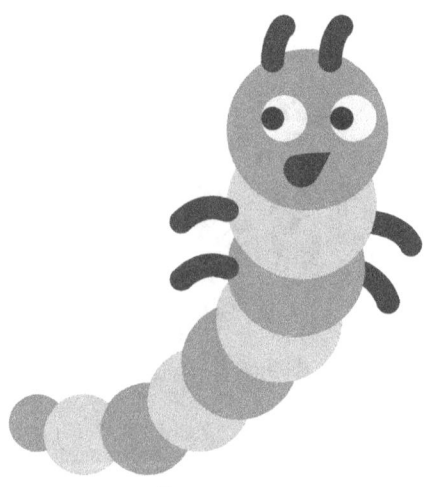
Inchworm

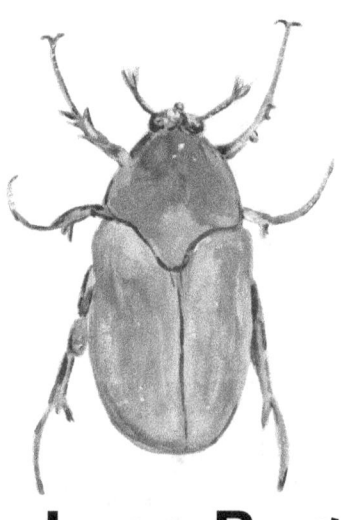
June Bug

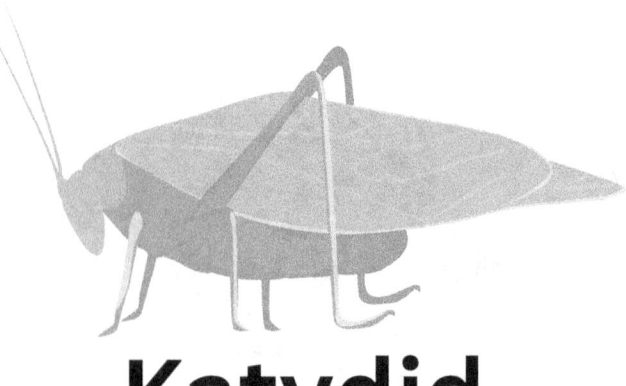
Katydid

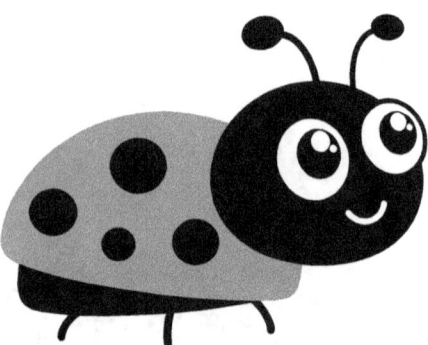
Ladybug

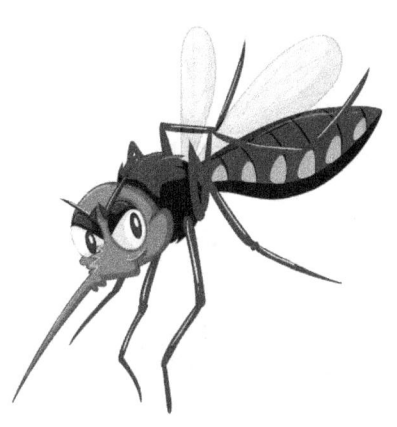

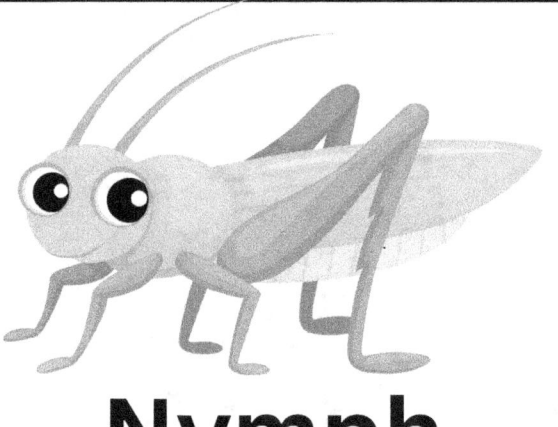

Nymph

Mosquito

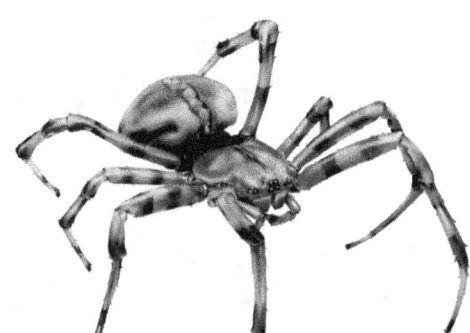

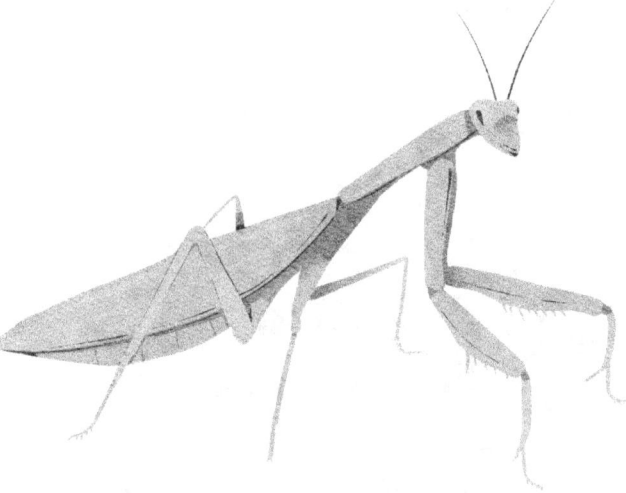

Orb-weaver Spider

Praying Mantis

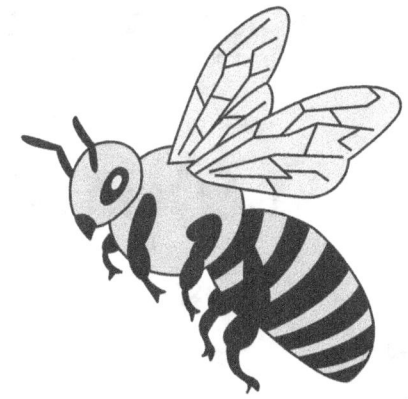

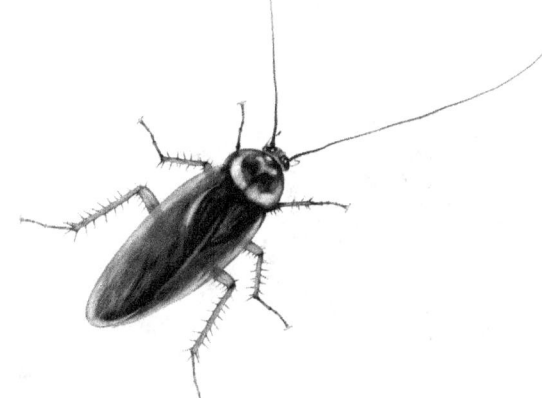

Roach

Queen Bee

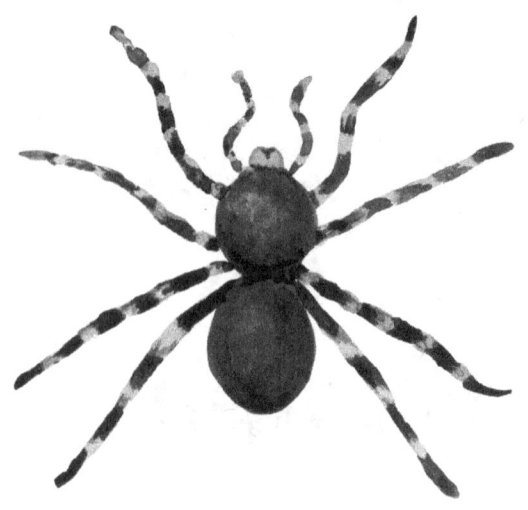
Spider

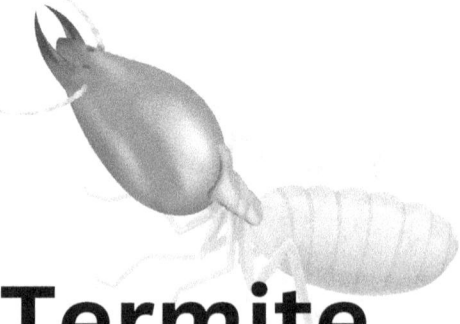
Termite

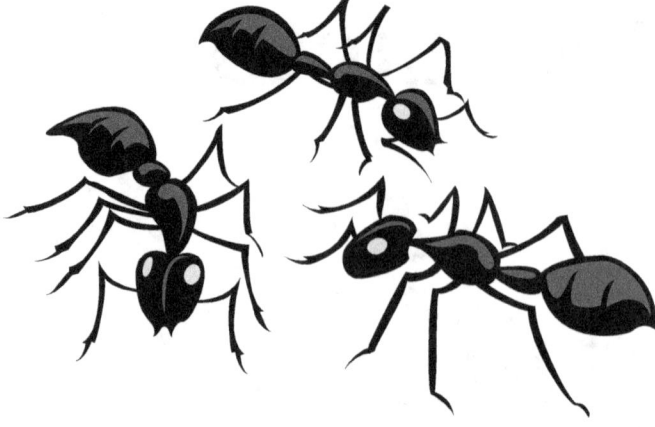
Velvet Ant

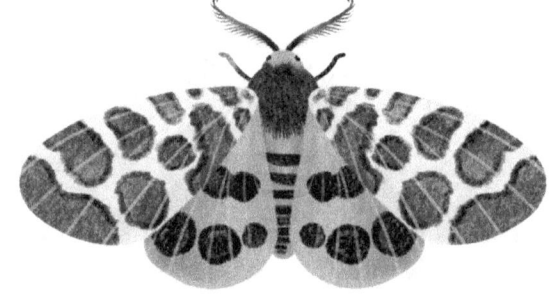
Underwing Moth

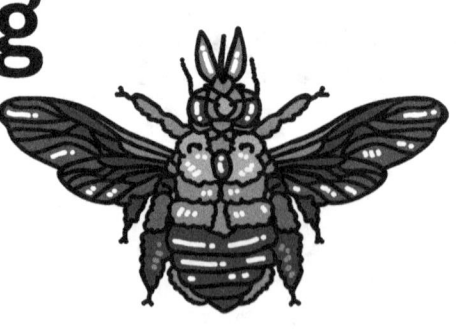
Xylocopa

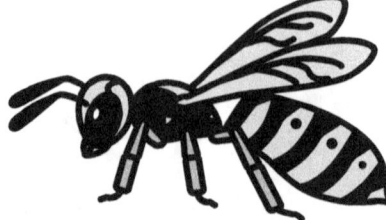
Yellowjacket

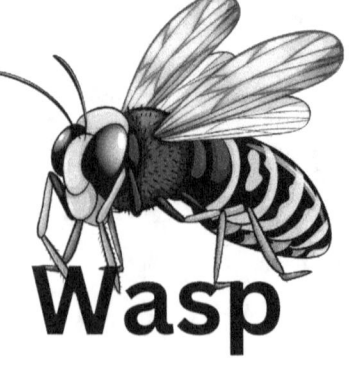
Wasp

Zebra Longwing Butterfly